Beginning

for adults

The Grown-Up Approach to Playing Bass

DAVE OVERTHROW

Music typesetting: Ante Gelo
CD recorded at Bar None Studio, Northford, CT
Cover photograph: Tim Becker/Creative Images Photography
Bass guitar on cover courtesy of Timothy Phelps
"Alta" (Siberian husky) courtesy of Calvin A. Bensch II
Special thanks to the LaGattuta family for the use of their home.

Alfred Music Publishing Co., Inc.
P.O. Box 10003
Van Nuys, CA 91410-0003
alfred.com

ISBN-10: 0-7390-9307-X (Book & CD)
ISBN-13: 978-0-7390-9307-8 (Book & CD)

Contents

Track 1

A compact disc is available for this book. This disc can make learning with the book easier and more enjoyable. The symbol shown to the left will appear next to every example that is on the CD. Use the CD to help ensure you are capturing the feel of the examples and interpreting the rhythms correctly. The track numbers below the symbols correspond directly to the example you want to hear. Track 1 will help you tune your bass to the CD.

Have fun!

About the Author

Dave Overthrow has been a bass performer and instructor since 1980. He studied at Berklee College of Music and later earned a degree in Jazz Performance from Western Connecticut State University. Dave has authored seven bass books, all published by Alfred Music Publishing. In addition to being the Director of Music and Head of Jazz Studies at the Canterbury School in New Milford, Connecticut, Dave is a staff writer for *Bass Guitar* magazine and teaches at his private studio. He regularly records and performs with his band, HipPocket, in New York and Connecticut and has recently finished his own CD entitled "In the Pocket."

For more about Dave Overthrow and his music, check out:

www.daveoverthrow.com

OTHER INSTRUCTIONAL PRODUCTS BY DAVE OVERTHROW
- *The Complete Electric Bass Method*
  Beginning Electric Bass (#19362)
  Intermediate Electric Bass (#19359)
  Mastering Electric Bass (#19356)
- *30 Day Bass Workout* (#20398)
- *Slap & Pop Bass* (#21904)
- *Beginning Blues Bass* (#22561)

PHOTO BY HEIDI JOHNSON

ACKNOWLEDGEMENTS
Thanks to Dave Smolover, Nat Gunod, Ron Blake for the incredible instruments he has built for me, the people at SWR Sound and DR Handmade Bass Strings. Thanks to Jim Lynch and Kurt Burgland for playing guitar and drums on the CD for this book. I would also like to thank my mother, the rest of my family and especially my wife Yvette.

Introduction

Welcome to *Beginning Bass for Adults*. The electric bass is a fun instrument to play and I am glad you have chosen it as your instrument. Thanks for choosing this book to help you get started and build a strong foundation for your bass playing.

The focus of this book is to enable you to play music with others. As a bass player, you need to know about your instrument, bass technique and music theory, such as the structure of chords. When you put these together, you can enjoy playing bass and play tunes on your own and with others.

This book teaches bass from the very beginning and makes it easy to learn. You'll learn some easy bass lines that you can use when playing in a group situation. Bass lines in a variety of styles, including blues, rock, funk and reggae are found throughout the book.

After this book you can move on and concentrate on styles such as blues or funk by picking up my other books, *Slap & Pop Bass* or *Beginning Blues Bass*. If you wish to learn more about chords, scales and how to create your own bass lines in many styles of music, you can pick up the *Complete Electric Bass Method* series. To learn about music theory in general and do some ear training, check out *Beginning Theory for Adults* (#40269).

 ## How to Use This Book

You can use this book in several ways. Chapter Three will teach you to read standard music notation. It will also help you learn the fretboard of your bass, which is necessary to becoming a good bassist. You can go through the chapters in order, or when you get to Chapter Three, you can also look ahead to later chapters to work on bass lines in various styles, such as blues and funk. From Chapter Six on, tablature (TAB) is provided for all of the bass lines. So, you can work on learning the fretboard and music notation while also working on learning bass lines from other parts of the book. A CD is available too. It includes demonstrations of all of the examples performed by the author and a professional band.

If you already have a teacher, they will help you choose what to work on; if not, the book is very user friendly and you can determine how to work through it yourself.

Chapter One

Buying Your Bass

It's time! You have decided to enter the world of electric bass guitar. Learning to play the bass can help you relax and experience the joy of playing music with old friends, new friends and even people you have never met. Buying your first bass guitar should be a pleasant experience. There are many basses to choose from, but we can narrow the field as far as which type of bass guitar you want to purchase by making a few decisions.

Most of us who choose to play the electric bass usually have one or more favorite artists that they want to emulate. If you grew up listening to Led Zeppelin, you probably want a bass that is capable of getting the John Paul Jones sound. Or, if you loved the sound of the bass on recordings by Yes, you'll want a bass like Chris Squire's (he plays a Rickenbacker).

Although there are many brands and models to choose from, we will discuss the two most popular types of basses: the "Jazz bass," otherwise known as the "J-bass;" and the precision bass, otherwise known as the "P-bass," both made by Fender. The "J-bass" has a thinner neck and a two pickup configuration, with a neck pickup and a bridge pickup. The neck pickup is the *bass* pickup (it gets a full, dark sound) and the bridge pickup is the *treble* pickup (it gets a thinner, brighter sound). The "P-bass" has a different pickup configuration. Both are located halfway between the neck and bridge. The "P-bass" pickup configuration results in a more "deep-end" sound. Generally, the "P-bass" is used for rock and the "J-bass" is used for funk and jazz.

Although the Jazz and Precision basses are the most common, there are many other good brands, such as Ibanez, Yamaha and too many more to mention. Most basically simulate the "J-" or "P-bass" or fall somewhere in between.

If you already have a teacher, or a friend that plays bass, it is a good idea to get some feedback from them. Bring them along to the nearest reputable dealer and have the salesperson demonstrate a bass. Tell the salesperson what type of music you are interested in and look for the bass that best fits the sound you are looking for. When trying the bass, press the strings to the fretboard and make sure you can do this with ease. If it is difficult or makes your hand uncomfortable to play, it probably isn't the bass for you.

Also, have a price range in mind. You don't have to spend a lot of money to get a bass that sounds good and is comfortable to play. Ask the salesperson to explore all options for basses in your price range.

It is a good idea to go with a brand that many of your friends play. Also, make sure the bass you buy has a warranty, repair and/or exchange policy.

Amplifiers

When you have decided on the bass you want to buy, it's time to get an amplifier (affectionately known as an "amp"). Like the bass, your choice of amp will depend mostly on the style of music you are interested in playing. Another important factor is whether you are going to use the amp to practice alone or to play with other musicians, such as a drummer. If you are going to play with a drummer, you will need to get an amp capable of getting the volume needed to be heard over the drums. Another factor is, of course, your price range.

Keep in mind that the physical size does not necessarily dictate the volume or quality of sound that will come out of the amp. There are many powerful amps that are fairly small. Go by the "specs," not the physical size. Once again, ask the advice of the salesperson, your friends and your teacher for an amp that will best suit your needs. In the "specs," the *wattage* will tell you how powerful the amp is, but also talk to the salesperson about the size of the speaker and the tone controls available on the amp. You want at least bass, *midrange* and *treble* tone controls, or an equalizer to boost and cut certain *frequencies*. *Frequency* is the *pitch*, or degree of highness or lowness, of the sound determined by the number of vibrations per second.

Parts of the Bass

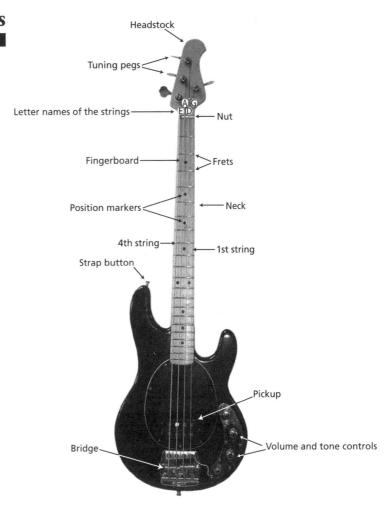

Holding the Bass

It should feel comfortable to hold the bass. Although most basses are a bit "neck heavy," the neck should be pointed up towards the ceiling so your left hand has access to the entire neck. If you let the neck dip down, it will be very difficult to play.

There are two basic positions for playing the bass: seated and standing.

Seated

Keeping the neck of the bass in an upward position, sit straight up and don't "slouch" or "hunch" over the bass. This will keep your muscles poised and ready to play and minimize excess tension. The longer you play, you will become aware of the many reasons that this is beneficial to playing the instrument more effectively.

Standing

To play the bass standing up, you need a strap. As with playing the bass seated, the neck should be in an upward position. Experiment wearing the bass at different "heights." Some players wear the bass extremely low, below their waist, and others wear the bass extremely high. It is best to start with the bass just above your waist and make adjustments from that height to find the most comfortable position. It is best if the bass is situated similarly to your seated position.

The Left Hand

The Left-Hand Fingers

The left-hand fingers are indicated as follows:

1 = 1st finger = Index
2 = 2nd finger = Middle
3 = 3rd finger = Ring
4 = 4th finger = Pinky

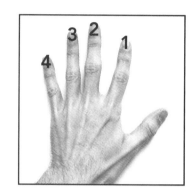

Left-Hand Position

The function of the left hand is to press the strings to the appropriate frets to produce the desired pitches. Correct left-hand positioning is essential to producing a good, clear tone.

The thumb of your left hand should be positioned on the back of the neck of your bass pointing upward. Make sure your thumb is sitting "flat" against the neck, right behind your 2nd finger.

Your finger should press the string down just to the left of the fret. This will help produce the best sounding tone. If you press the string down in the middle of the fret you may create some fret buzzing.

Fingers should be curled at both knuckles and the fingertips should press the strings down to the frets.

Your wrist should be bent towards the floor to allow your hand to arch in front of the fretboard. There should be a gap between your palm and the neck of the bass. Your palm should not touch the neck.

Your fingernails need to be trimmed to play the bass effectively. Long fingernails will prevent your fingertips from pressing the strings to the frets to produce notes.

The Right Hand

The right hand should be as relaxed as possible. Most players pluck the strings with their index and middle fingers. A commonly used technique is the *rest stroke*, executed by planting the finger on the string, pulling it sharply across and landing on the adjacent string. After you feel comfortable playing notes with your index finger with this technique, try it with your middle finger and then practice alternating fingers. Again, most bass players use both fingers.

The thumb can be anchored on the pickup when playing the 4th (lowest) string.

It can be rested on the 4th string when playing the 3rd, 2nd or 1st strings.

Here is the index finger preparing to pluck the 1st string.

Here is the index finger after plucking the 1st string.

Here is the index finger after plucking the 4th string. Notice the difference because there is no string to rest on.

Tuning Your Bass

It is very important for your bass to be in tune, otherwise your playing won't sound pleasing to the ears. There are several ways you can tune your bass. You can use a pitchpipe, an electronic tuner or the traditional method, which is to tune the bass by ear. This is called *relative tuning* and is covered on page 13.

Pitch Pipe

A pitch pipe gives you a pitch to match each string. The pitch pipe has individual pipes that correspond to the strings. You can use a violin pitch pipe, which has the right notes for the bass, or the bottom four pitches of a guitar pitch pipe. Keep in mind that the pitch pipe will sound an octave or two above each of the strings you will be tuning. Just blow into the pipe and match the corresponding string to the sound.

Electronic Tuner (Highly Recommended)

An electronic tuning device can be very helpful for those who are not yet comfortable with the relative tuning method. They are relatively inexpensive and are the best choice for beginning players since they are easy to use and will help train your musical ear. As you gain experience playing in tune, you will gradually find the relative tuning method easy to do.

Track 1

You can also tune to Track 1 of the CD that is available for this book.

**Martin, 51
Home Improvement**

"I love the sound of the bass and play purely for the fun of it. I love Rocco Prestia of Tower of Power. There is nothing more enjoyable than playing funk grooves with a drummer."

Relative Tuning

Relative tuning is the process of tuning your bass by ear. Though it might be difficult to do at first, with practice and patience it will become easy. The time it takes to develop your musical ear enough to tune by ear varies from person to person. The process is described below.

1) First, tune your open 4th string E to a *tuning fork* (E tuning forks are available at many music stores), pitch pipe, keyboard or an in-tune bass or guitar. On a keyboard, use the E that is nineteen white keys below middle C (see diagram below).

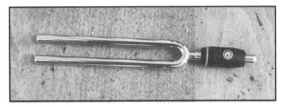

Tuning fork.

2) To tune your 3rd string, place a finger on the 5th fret of the 4th string to produce the note A. The open 3rd string should match this note. If not, use the tuning peg for the 3rd string to tighten the string (if it is too low, *flat*) or loosen it (if the string is too high, *sharp*).

3) To tune your 2nd string, place a finger on the 5th fret of the 3rd string to produce the note D. The open 2nd string should match this note. If not, use the tuning peg for the 2nd string to adjust it.

4) To tune your 1st string, place a finger on the 5th fret of the 2nd string to produce the note G. The open 1st string should match this note. If not, use the tuning peg for the 1st string to adjust it.

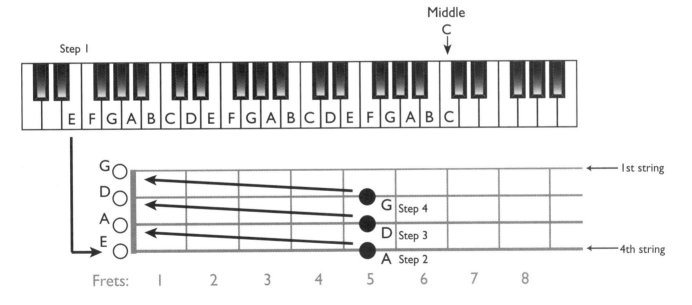

Chapter Two

One of the rewards of being able to read standard music notation is that it can open the doors for you to be exposed to music from all over the world. A musician can experience playing music written by musicians of any country, from any time.

Reading standard notation also allows you communicate ideas quickly with other musicians. If you write songs and want other musicians to play them, standard music notation helps you to express your ideas and have them understood.

Songbooks that you buy in music stores will use standard music notation, and if you can read pitch and rhythms—the language of music—you can buy these books and play songs from your favorite artists.

 ## Reading Music—Pitch

The Staff
Music is written on a *staff*, which has five lines and four spaces and is read from left to right.

Clef
At the beginning of the staff is the *clef*. Music for bass is written in the *bass clef*, sometimes called the *F clef* because whichever line its two dots surround is called "F."

Musical Alphabet
The lines and spaces of the staff and musical pitches have letter names taken from the musical alphabet, which has seven letters that repeat: A B C D E F G, A B C etc. *Notes* placed on the staff are given the name of the line or space on which they appear and tell us which pitch to play. You can remember the notes on the lines with the phrase, **G**ood **B**assists **D**o **F**unk **A**lways. You can remember the notes on the spaces with the phrase, **A**ll **C**ows **E**at **G**rass.

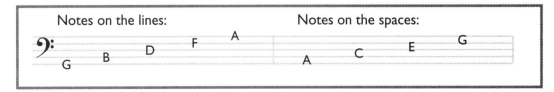

Notes

Notes are placed on the staff to tell us which pitch to play, when to play it and how long it lasts. Here are some notes and their parts.

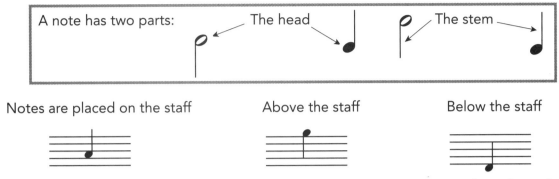

Notes are placed on the staff   Above the staff   Below the staff

Notes with stems on or above the 3rd, center line have the stems going down from the left. Notes below the 3rd line have the stems going up from the right.

The letter name of a note is determined by what line or space it occupies on the staff. For example, this is a G note because the note occupies the G space on the staff.

Reading Music—Time

The type of note tells us how long a pitch should last. Here are three important note values:

o This is a **whole note**. The head is hollow and has no stem.

These are **half notes**. A half note has a stem and a hollow head. Two half notes equal one whole note.

These are **quarter notes**. A quarter note has a stem and a solid head. Two quarter notes equal one half note.

Each type of note has a specific duration measured in beats. A beat is the basic unit of musical time. When you tap your foot to music, you are tapping the beats. Here is a diagram showing the values normally attributed to the notes you just learned.

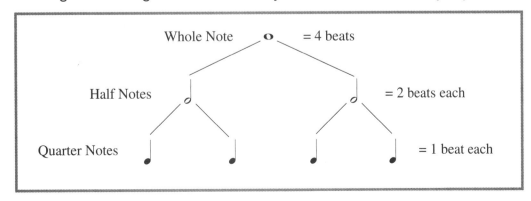

Measures and Barlines

The staff is divided into *measures* by vertical lines called *barlines*. Because of the barlines, musicians will often call a measure a "bar." Each measure contains a specific number of beats.

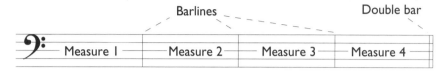

A *double bar* marks the end of a short example or section.

Rests

Each type of note we have covered has a corresponding duration of silence known as a *rest*. A whole rest normally indicates four beats of silence, a half rest indicates two beats of silence and the quarter rest indicates one beat of silence.

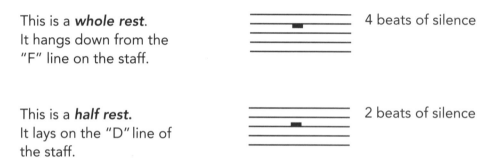

This is a **whole rest**.
It hangs down from the
"F" line on the staff.

4 beats of silence

This is a **half rest**.
It lays on the "D" line of
the staff.

2 beats of silence

Notice that whole note and half note rests look similar. The difference is that the whole rest hangs from a line while the half rest sits on a line.

This is a **quarter rest**.

1 beat of silence

Time Signatures

At the beginning of any piece of music, you'll find a *time signature*. A time signature consists of two numbers, one on top of the other. The top number indicates how many beats are in each measure. The bottom number tells you what kind of note gets one beat, and is usually a four, representing a quarter note. Here is the most common time signature:

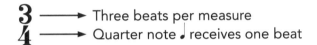

$\frac{4}{4}$ time is so common it is often called *common time* and indicated with this symbol: **C**.

When playing music in $\frac{4}{4}$, count like this: "1, 2, 3, 4, 1, 2, 3, 4," and so on.

Count: 1 2 3 4   1 2 3 4   1 2 3 4   1 2 3 4

Here are some other commonly found time signatures:

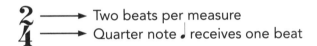

Bill, 35
School bus driver

Bill likes rock 'n' roll bass players and loves to get together with guitarists to work on songs.

Chapter Two

Chapter Three
lesson 1: the open strings

Here are the open strings of the bass shown in standard music notation.

The Open String Notes

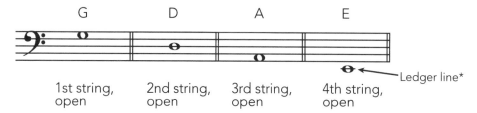

1st string, open   2nd string, open   3rd string, open   4th string, open

* *Ledger lines* are an extension of the staff. They allow you to write notes both above and below the staff. One reason this is important is that the lowest note on the bass (the 4th string, E) is too low to be written on the staff.

When playing the open string studies it is important to:

1) Alternate the index and middle fingers of the right hand.

2) Stop the sound of each note when its duration has expired. Stop the vibration of the string by touching it with the fingers of the left or right hand.

It is common for bassists to alternate the index and middle fingers of the right hand to pluck the strings. If a fingering is given in this book, it does not have to be followed to the letter. The fingering shown is a suggestion and you can change it if you like. For example, the first study indicates to begin the alternation with the index finger. Try starting with the middle finger and see which works best for you.

Though most bass players use the fingers of the right hand to pluck the strings, some use a pick. When playing with a pick, it is a good idea to alternate *downstrokes* (toward the floor) and *upstrokes* (toward the ceiling).

We will use the following symbols to indicate right-hand fingerings:

  ⊓ = Index finger or downstroke

  V = Middle finger or upstroke

Whole Note Study

In $\frac{4}{4}$ time a whole note receives four beats. A whole note is struck on the first beat and sustained for the remaining three.

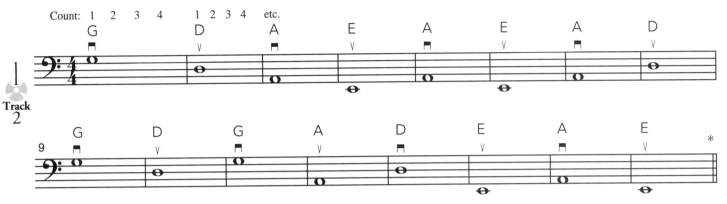

* The double bar indicates the end of the piece.

Half Note Study

The half note receives two beats. It is struck on the first beat and sustained for the second. When playing this study, try to stop each note from ringing when its duration expires, otherwise more than one pitch will be sounding at the same time.

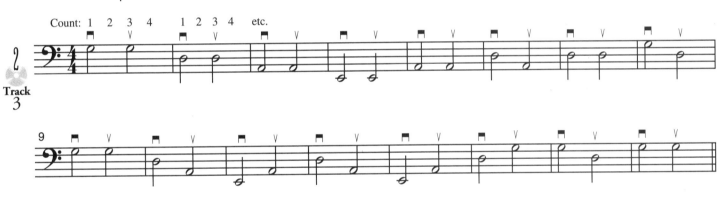

Quarter Note Study

Play this example slowly at first. Count carefully.

lesson 2: notes on the 1st string

Use the 1st and 3rd fingers of the left hand to play the A and B notes.

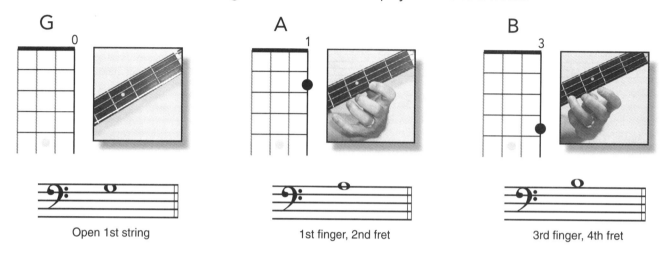

G — Open 1st string
A — 1st finger, 2nd fret
B — 3rd finger, 4th fret

Remember to alternate fingers of the right hand when playing the following studies.

Whole and Half Note Study

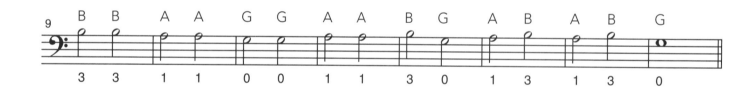

Half and Quarter Note Study

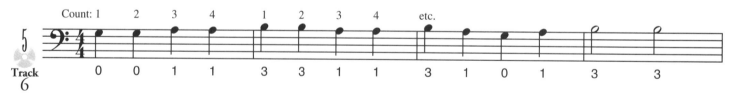

Beginning Bass for Adults

Dotted Half Note

A dot to the right of a note increases its value by one half. Since a half note equals two beats (2), a *dotted half note* receives three beats (2+1=3).

Half note = 2 beats   The dot is worth half the value = 1

$$\text{♩} \;+\; \centerdot \;=\; \text{♩}\centerdot$$
$$2 \;+\; 1 \qquad 3$$

¾ Time

In ¾ time there are three beats per measure and the quarter note receives one beat.

3 Beats per measure
4 Quarter note ♩ receives one beat

Track 7

Triple Treat

Count: 1   2   3   1   2   3   etc.

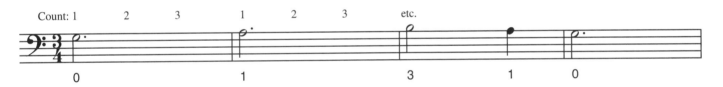

0   1   3   1   0

3   1   0   1   3   1   0

0   1   3   3   1   0   3   1   0

3   1   3   1   0   1   3   0

Chapter Three

The next tune uses the quarter rest you learned on page 16. As you know, it indicates one beat of silence. Use the left or right hand to stop the string from ringing to produce a quarter note rest.

 = Quarter rest. One beat of silence.

Notice the different combinations of note values that appear in this study. Count carefully and keep a steady beat.

Practice the tune slowly at first and then gradually pick up the *tempo* (speed). After you have practiced on your own, practice the study with the CD that is available with this book.

Make sure to stop the string from ringing for the quarter note rests. To get the full effect of the quarter note rest, release the finger from the fretboard (but not the string).

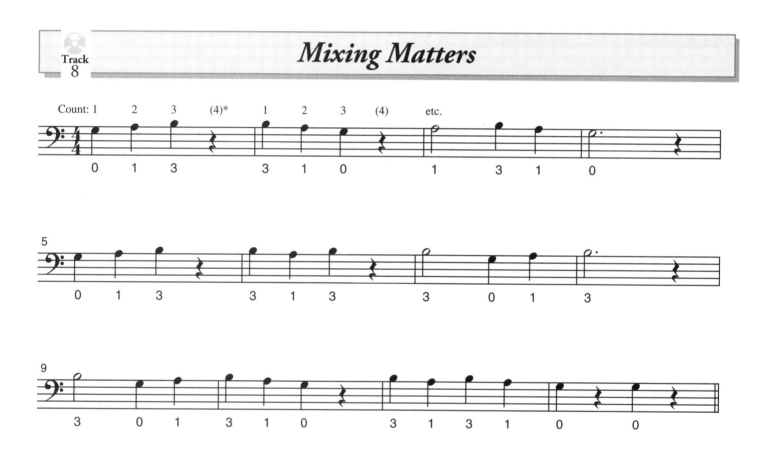

* Numbers in parentheses correspond to rests in the music. They are used to assist in counting beats.

lesson 3: notes on the 2nd string

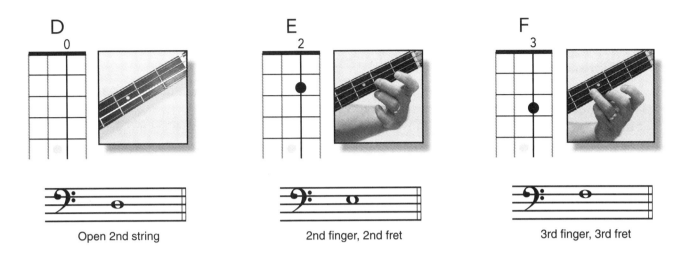

D — Open 2nd string
E — 2nd finger, 2nd fret
F — 3rd finger, 3rd fret

Whole and Half Note Study

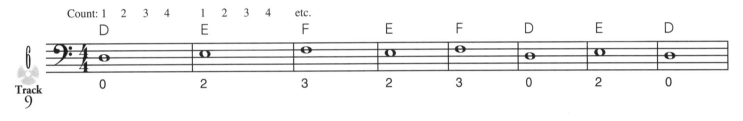

Half and Quarter Note Study

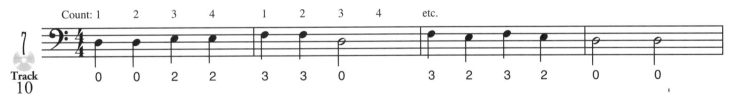

Chapter Three

Notes on the 1st and 2nd String

Half Notes

Although the F note (first and seventh measure, 3rd beat) is usually played with the 3rd finger, in this example it makes more sense to play it with the 2nd finger. This will make it easier to play the A and B notes in the second measure with the 1st and 3rd fingers.

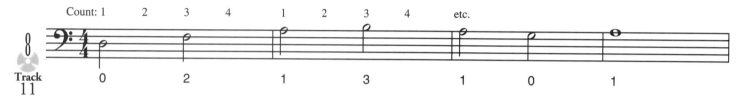

Half Notes and Quarter Notes

In this example, it makes sense to play the A note with your 2nd finger instead of the 1st finger.

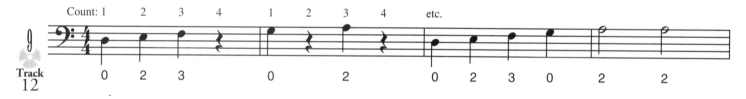

Beginning Bass for Adults

lesson 4: notes on the 3rd string

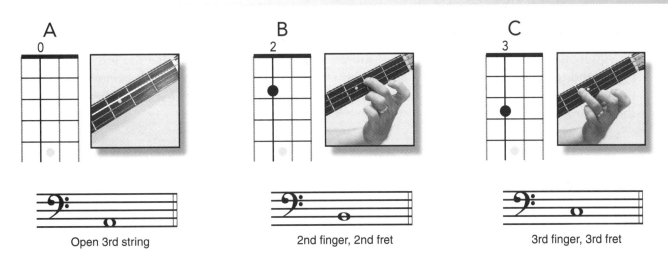

Open 3rd string   2nd finger, 2nd fret   3rd finger, 3rd fret

Whole and Half Note Study

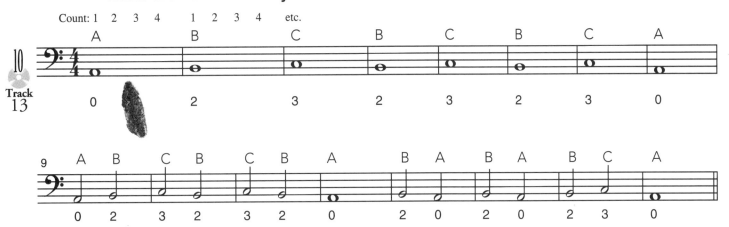

Half and Quarter Note Study

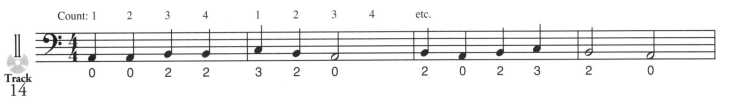

Notes on the 1st, 2nd and 3rd Strings

As you learned on page 16, the half rest indicates two beats of silence. Use the left or right hand to stop the string from ringing. Remember, the half rest is similar looking to the whole rest, but it sits on the 3rd line (D) of the staff and the whole rest hangs from the 4th line (F).

 = Half rest. Two beats of silence.

This study below is a reggae bass line played on three strings. Notice the half note rests.

Track 15

Three-String Reggae

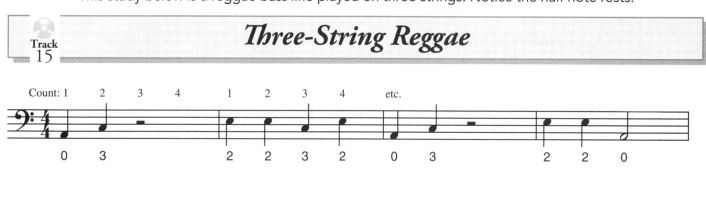

Beginning Bass for Adults

lesson 5: notes on the 4th string

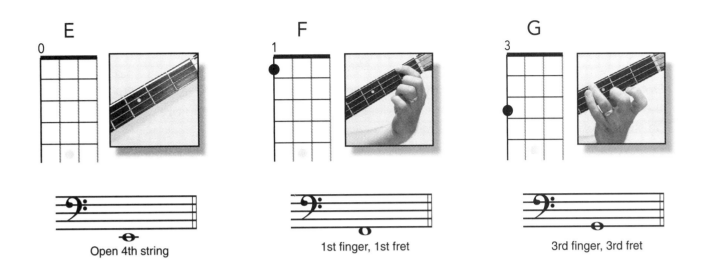

Open 4th string

1st finger, 1st fret

3rd finger, 3rd fret

Whole and Half Note Study

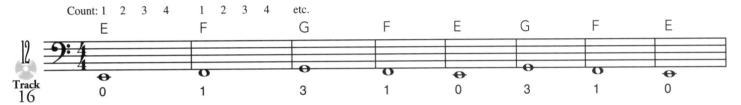

Half and Quarter Note Study

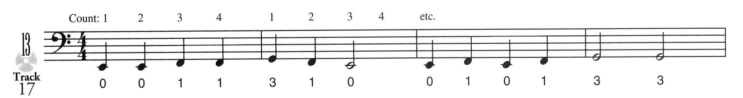

Notes on All Four Strings

As you learned on page 16, the whole rest indicates four beats of silence.

Do not confuse the whole note rest with the half note rest. They may look similar but the whole note rest hangs from the F note line on the staff while the half note rest sits on the D note line.

= Whole rest. Four beats of silence.

In "All Four One," it is best to play the A note on the 2nd fret of the 1st string (bars 1 and 9) with the 2nd finger.

Track 18

All Four One

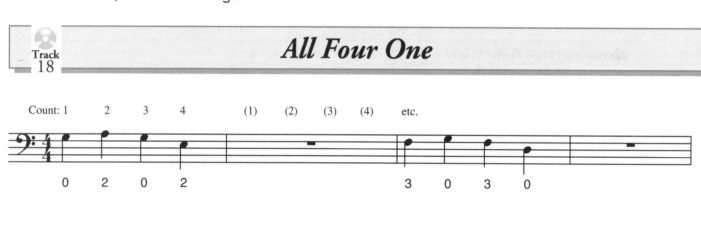

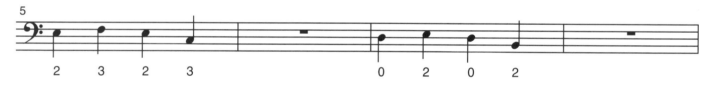

High C

The high C note is played by placing the 4th finger at the 5th fret of the 1st string. If you wish, when playing a note with the 4th finger, you can use the other fingers as support by pressing them to the fretboard. The 4th finger is the weakest and this makes it easier to use. Also, if you slightly turn your hand, moving the 4th finger closer to the neck, it will give you more leverage and may make it easier to produce the note.

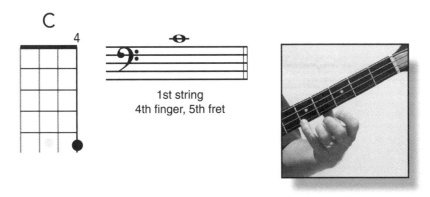

1st string
4th finger, 5th fret

lesson 6: the major scale

A *scale* is a series of notes with a specific arrangement of *whole steps* and *half steps*.

- A half step is a distance of one fret.

- A whole step is a distance of two half steps or two frets.

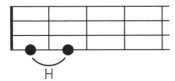

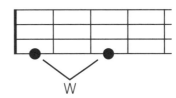

The *major scale* is the most important and most commonly used scale. It can be played starting on any note, which is then called the *tonic*, and then proceeding through the musical alphabet with the following arrangement of whole steps (W) and half steps (H): W–W–H–W–W–W–H. This formula is very important and should be memorized.

The scale takes the name of the tonic note. For example, a major scale built on the note C is the *C Major scale*.

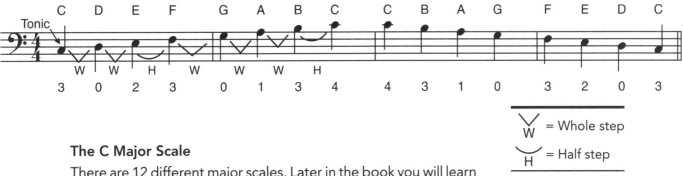

The C Major Scale
There are 12 different major scales. Later in the book you will learn some of the more commonly used major scales.

Keep in mind that you should work out right-hand fingerings while playing the following pieces. It is best to alternate fingers.

C Major Scale Exercise 1

A *melodic pattern* is a short melody, usually three or four notes, with a distinctive shape that is repeated. This one is three notes ascending stepwise followed by a descending skip.

C Major Melodic Pattern

C Major Scale Exercise 2—Major Scale Melody

The Tie

A *tie* is a curved line between two notes of the same pitch. The first note is played and held for the duration of both. The second note is not struck. Rather, its value is added to that of the first.

The tie often occurs over a barline.

Terrific Ties

Track 22

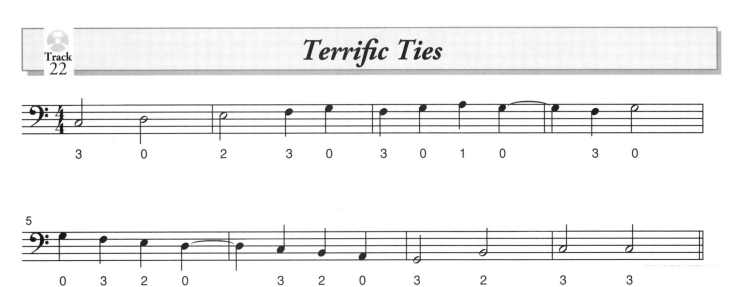

Towering Ties

Track 23

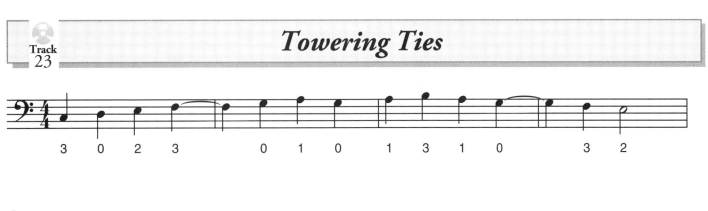

Chapter Three

The Repeat Sign

Two dots with one thin and one heavy line at the end of a piece of music comprise a *repeat sign*, which tells you to repeat the music from the beginning.

Repeat sign

Notice the *chord symbols* in the pieces below. They are there so an accompanist can play chords as you play the bass part. It is helpful to have a friend or teacher play along so you can hear how the bass part sounds against the chords. The chords are played on the CD that is available for this book.

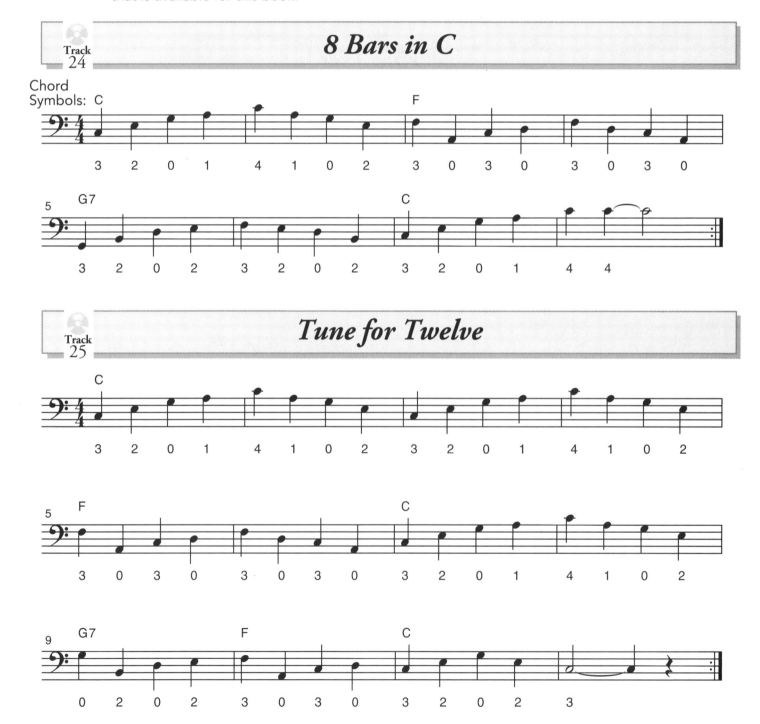

Eighth Notes

An eighth note receives half a beat. The head is solid, there is a stem and a flag.

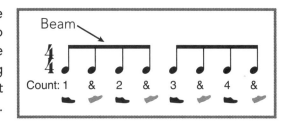

Flag
= ½ beat

Two eighth notes equal one quarter note.

♪ ♪ = ♩

Consecutive eighth notes are beamed together and are counted like this: "1–&, 2–&, 3–&, 4–&." There are two parts to every beat. When you tap your foot, there are two parts to the movement: the part where you bring your foot up (the *offbeat*), and the part where you bring it down (the *onbeat*). Each of these parts is an eighth note.

Beam
$\frac{4}{4}$
Count: 1 & 2 & 3 & 4 &

When playing eighth notes, you should consistently alternate the right-hand index and middle fingers.

Track 26

Eight to the Bar

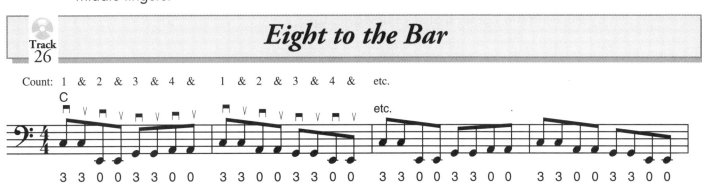

Count: 1 & 2 & 3 & 4 & 1 & 2 & 3 & 4 & etc.

etc.

3 3 0 0 3 3 0 0   3 3 0 0 3 3 0 0   3 3 0 0 3 3 0 0   3 3 0 0 3 3 0 0

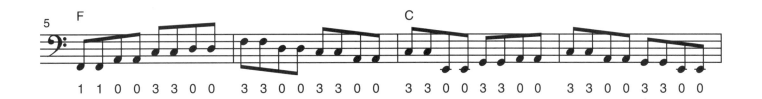

1 1 0 0 3 3 0 0   3 3 0 0 3 3 0 0   3 3 0 0 3 3 0 0   3 3 0 0 3 3 0 0

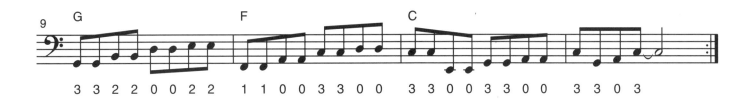

3 3 2 2 0 0 2 2   1 1 0 0 3 3 0 0   3 3 0 0 3 3 0 0   3 3 0 3

Chapter Three

The Eighth Rest

Like an eighth note, the *eighth rest* gets a ½ beat.

𝄾 = ½ beat of silence

Eighth Rest Exercise

Here is an easy reggae bass line that contains a few eighth rests. Remember to create the rest by stopping the vibration of any ringing string.

Rasta Riff

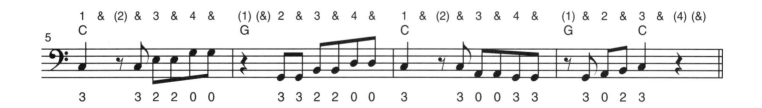

Beginning Bass for Adults

Chapter Four

Accidentals

Accidentals are signs used to raise, lower or return a pitch to its original pitch.

♯ SHARP

This sign raises the note a half step (one fret). For example, the note A is located on the 2nd fret of the 1st string, so A♯ (*A-sharp*) is located on the 3rd fret. When a note is sharped, it remains sharped for the entire measure.

♭ FLAT

This sign lowers the note a half step (one fret). For example, the note A is located on the 2nd fret of the 1st string, so A♭ (*A-flat*) is located on the 1st fret. When a note is flatted, it remains flatted for the entire measure.

♮ NATURAL

All notes without sharps or flats are *natural notes*. This symbol is used to indicate the change from a previously sharped or flatted note to a natural pitch. In other words, it cancels any previous sharp or flat within the measure. A barline also cancels a sharp or flat. Accidentals are only in effect for the measure in which they occur.

1st String Accidentals

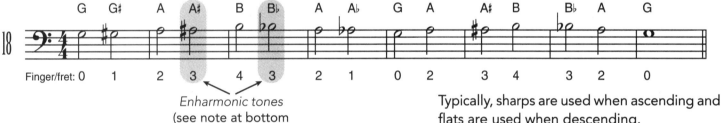

Enharmonic tones (see note at bottom of page)

Typically, sharps are used when ascending and flats are used when descending.

2nd String Accidentals

3rd String Accidentals

4th String Accidentals

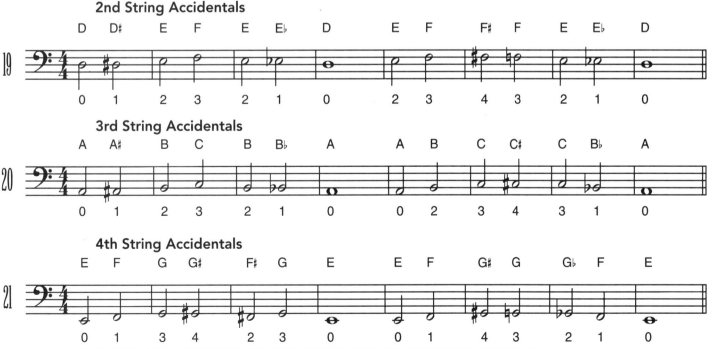

Every sharp note (for example, A♯, 3rd fret, 1st string) can also be expressed as a flat note (B♭, 3rd fret, 1st string). Two notes of the same pitch with different names are called *enharmonic* tones.

Key Signatures—
The Key of G Major

A *key* is the tonal center of a composition. If music is written with the notes of the C Major scale, it is in the *key of C Major*. A *key signature* is a group of sharps or flats (never both) at the beginning of a line of music. It tells us which key the piece is in and which notes to play sharp or flat throughout the piece. If a note is altered in the key signature, accidentals are not needed for that note in the music (except perhaps to temporarily cancel the key signature with a natural sign). Thus far, all of the music you have played in this book has been in the key of C Major. Let's learn a different key.

The Key of G

In the key of G all F's are sharped and are indicated in the key signature.

Key signature

You need to learn these notes on the bass to play the G Major scale.

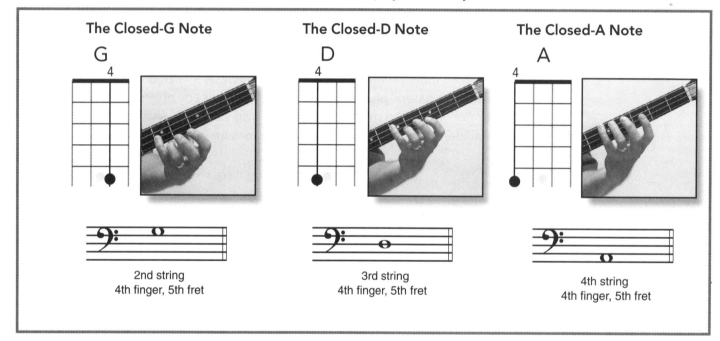

The Closed-G Note
G
4

2nd string
4th finger, 5th fret

The Closed-D Note
D
4

3rd string
4th finger, 5th fret

The Closed-A Note
A
4

4th string
4th finger, 5th fret

G Major Scale

G Major Scale Exercise

Beginning Bass for Adults

Play these lines slowly at first.

3 Chords in G

Track 30

Remember to alternate the right-hand fingers when playing eighth notes. Strive for an even sound, with each note matching the volume of the others. Count carefully.

Exercise in G Major

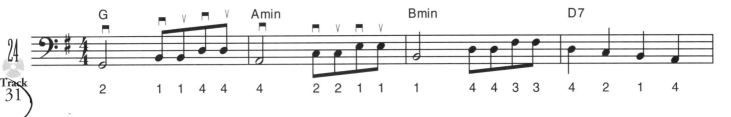

Track 31

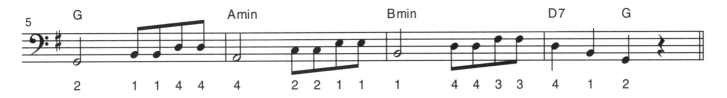

The Key of D Major

Notice that the D Major scale (example 25) has two sharps. In the D Major scale, all F and C notes are sharped.

You need to learn the high D note to play the D Major scale.

1st string
4th finger, 7th fret

D Major Scale

D   E   F♯   G   A   B   C♯   D

4   1   3   4   1 — 1   3   4   4   3   1 — 1   4   3   1   4

D Major Scale Exercise

Track 32

4   3   1   4   3   1   4   4   3   1   4   3   1   4

5

4   1   3   4   1   2   4   4   1   3   4   1   3   4

D Major Study

Notice the variety of rhythms in this study. Count carefully and alternate fingers in the right hand.

Count: 1 & 2 & 3 & 4 &   1 & 2 & 3 & 4 &   1 & 2 & 3 & 4 &   1 & 2 & 3 & 4 &

Track 33

4   0 1 2   4   2 4 1 3 4   4   1 3 4   1 — 1   3   4

1 & 2 & 3 & 4 &   1 & 2 & 3 & 4 &   1 & 2 & 3 & 4 &   1 & 2 & 3 & 4 &

5

4   3   1 — 1   4   1 4 3   3   4   1   3   4   1 3 4

Beginning Bass for Adults

Rock 'n' Roll Bass Line in D

Track 34

This bass line uses mostly eighth notes and is created on a common *chord progression* (series of chords) that you will learn about in Chapter Six. Remember to alternate the fingers in the right hand and count carefully.

Rockin' with Eighths in G

Track 35

Chapter Four

The Key of F Major

Notice that the key signature for F Major has one flat. In the F Major scale (example 28), all B notes are flatted.

F Major Scale

F Major Scale Exercise

Track 36

Track 37

Halves & Eighths in F

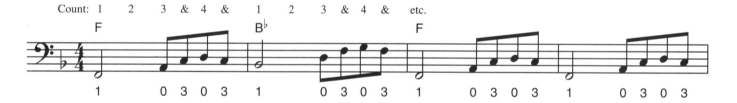

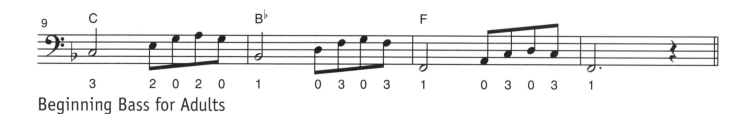

Beginning Bass for Adults

Dotted Quarter Note

A dot to the right of a note increases its value by one half. Since a quarter note equals one beat (1), a *dotted quarter note* receives 1½ beats (1+½=1½).

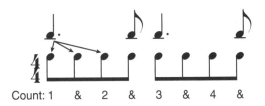

The dotted quarter note is equal to three eighth notes.

Count: 1 & 2 & 3 & 4 &

Bossa Nova

The *bossa nova* rhythm is a Latin dance rhythm commonly found in many styles of music. The characteristic rhythm of the bass part in a bossa nova groove is a dotted-quarter/eighth-note feel.

Count: 1 & 2 & 3 & 4 & 1 & 2 & 3 & 4 &

Here is a bossa nova bass line in the key of F Major.

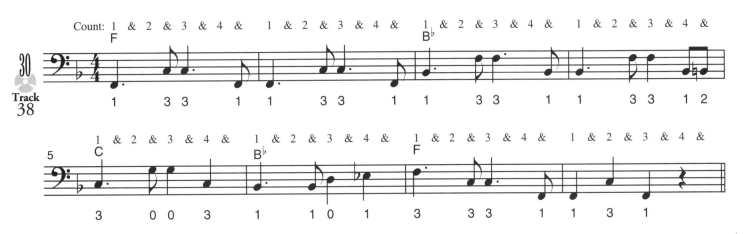

Review of G and F Major

Here is a boogie bass line in the key of G Major. This line might sound familiar to you. It can be heard on many tunes.

Boogie in G

Track 39

This boogie bass line is in the key of F Major, uses dotted quarter notes and is played over major chords.

Major Dots in F

Track 40

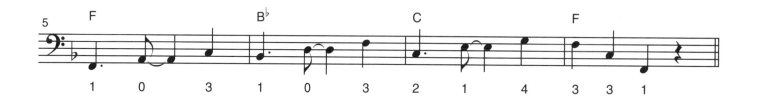

Beginning Bass for Adults

Cut Time

Most of the music you have played in this book up to this point has been in $\frac{4}{4}$, or common time.

Here is a symbol used to represent common time. Sometimes this symbol is used instead of the $\frac{4}{4}$ time signature.

C = common time $\frac{4}{4}$

Cut time feels like there are two beats per measure with the half note equaling one beat ($\frac{2}{2}$).

Here is the symbol for cut time: **¢**

Cut time usually indicates a quick tempo.

Track 41

Country Kid

The *samba*, like the bossa nova, is a popular Latin rhythm. Here is a samba bass line written in cut time.

Track 42

Samba in D

Chapter Four

Chapter Five

Sixteenth Notes

A *sixteenth note* receives one quarter of a beat.

♪ = ¼

Four sixteenth notes equal one quarter note.

In ⁴/₄ time, the most common time signature, there are 16 sixteenth notes per measure (hence the name). There are two sixteenth notes in each half beat (two sixteenth notes = one eighth note). Consecutive sixteenth notes are beamed together with double beams. Count "1–e–&–ah, 2–e–&–ah, 3–e–&–ah, 4–e–&–ah."

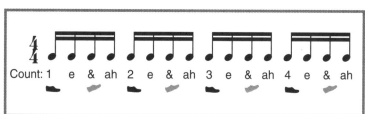

Count: 1 e & ah 2 e & ah 3 e & ah 4 e & ah

Following is a rock bass line using sixteenth notes. Remember to alternate your fingers.

Track 43

Rockin' the House in C

A *ballad* is a tune played at a slow tempo. Playing slower can actually be more difficult than playing fast. Concentrate on keeping a steady count when playing the sixteenth notes.

Note that the rhythm is similar to the bossa nova rhythm (page 41).

Track 44

Ballad in G

Funk music often uses sixteenth-note bass lines and is fun to play. Chapter Nine (page 83) discusses funk bass lines in detail, but let's get our feet wet with a couple of funk bass lines. Be sure to play this slowly at first and count very carefully.

Octaves

An *octave* is a distance of 12 half steps. Play a G note on the 3rd fret of your bass, then play up the G Major scale and stop on the 8th tone, which is also a G note. The ending G is an octave higher than the starting G. Octaves are commonly used in bass parts.

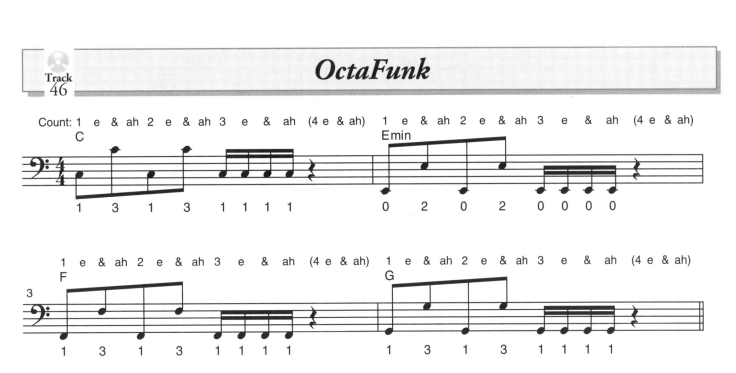

Dotted Eighth Note

As you know, a dot to the right of a note increases its value by one half. Since an eighth note equals half a beat (½, equal to two sixteenth notes), a *dotted eighth* note receives ¾ beats (½+¼ =¾).

$$\quad + \quad \cdot \quad = \quad$$
$$½ + ¼ \quad ¾$$

A dotted eighth note equals three sixteenth notes.

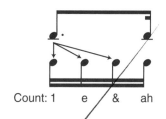

Count: 1 e & ah

It is common to find bass lines with the dotted eighth/sixteenth-note rhythm.

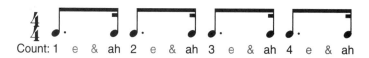

Count: 1 e & ah 2 e & ah 3 e & ah 4 e & ah

Here is a bass line using the dotted eighth/sixteenth-note rhythm. Remember to alternate the fingers of the right hand.

Dotted Eighth Note 8-Bar Blues in C

Track 47

Count: 1 e & ah 2 e & ah 3 e & ah 4 e & ah etc.

2   2 1   1 2   2 3   4   2   2 1   1 2   2 3   4

1   1 0   0 1   1 2   3   1   1 0   0 1   1 2   3

2   2 1   1 2   2 3   4   2   2 1   1 2   2 3   4

2   2 1   1 2   2 3   4   2   2   2

The Eighth-Note Triplet

An *eighth-note triplet* is a group of three eighth notes played in the same time of two. In other words, an eighth-note triplet is three equal notes in one beat. A triplet is usually indicated with the number "3."

When playing triplets it is helpful to count "1–&–ah, 2–&–ah, 3–&–ah,4–&–ah," or "1–trip–let, 2–trip–let, 3–trip–let, 4–trip–let."

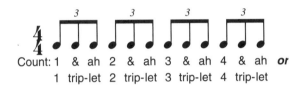

Count: 1 & ah 2 & ah 3 & ah 4 & ah **or**
1 trip-let 2 trip-let 3 trip-let 4 trip-let

Eighth-Note Triplet Blues

Track 48

Chapter Five

Chapter Six

Bass Tablature

Tablature, which we will call *TAB*, is used to indicate where notes are located on the fretboard. TAB was invented hundreds of years ago, before music for fretted instruments was written in standard music notation.

Here is how TAB works: The four lines represent the four strings of the bass—the top line is the 1st string (G), the bottom line is the 4th string; the numbers on the lines tell you which fret to play.

For example:

The numbers underneath show which left-hand fingers to use.

In the example above, the number 2 is on the top line, so the note is located on the 2nd fret of the 1st string. The number 3 is on the 2nd line, so this note is played on the 3rd fret of the 2nd string. The number 1 is located on the 3rd line, so this note is played on the 1st fret of the 3rd string.

For the remainder of this book, all examples and bass lines will be written in TAB with standard notation above it, which is the prevailing practice in books and magazines today. Use the standard music notation as much as possible, since it will give you the rhythms and clearly show silences (rests, which do not appear in TAB). The TAB is here to make it easier for you to enjoy the many examples while concentrating on the styles and techniques.

This portion of the book will introduce you to some commonly used chords, chord progressions and scale types commonly used by bassists to create great sounding bass lines. The emphasis will be on bass lines in the rock, blues, funk and reggae styles, which are some of the most enjoyable styles to play on the bass. Learning bass lines in these styles will help prepare you to play with your friends and many other musicians.

Some of the bass lines will be written in keys you have not yet studied, but being aware of the key signatures will allow you to play them. If you want to learn about the construction of chords and scales in more depth and how they apply to the bass, check out the *Beginning Electric Bass* (#19362) and *Musicianship for the Contemporary Bassist* (#21912).

Intervals of the Major Scale

An *interval* is the distance between two notes. Musicians often need to think about the relationships between notes.

If you measure the distance between the root of a major scale and each of the other notes in the scale, you get *major* and *perfect* intervals. The scale degrees 2, 3, 6 and 7 produce major intervals above the tonic. The scale degrees 4 and 5 are perfect intervals above the tonic.

Here are the intervals above a C tonic:

Interval Name: Perfect Unison   Major 2nd   Major 3rd   Perfect 4th   Perfect 5th   Major 6th   Major 7th   Perfect Octave

Intervals shown in the C Major scale.

Perfect Unison   Major 2nd   Major 3rd   Perfect 4th   Perfect 5th   Major 6th   Major 7th   Perfect Octave
Tonic

Major and Perfect Interval Practice

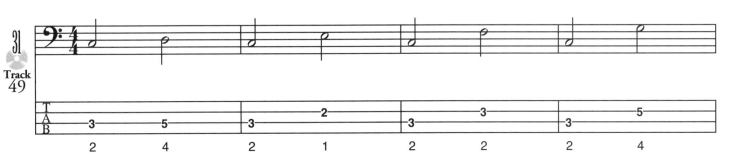

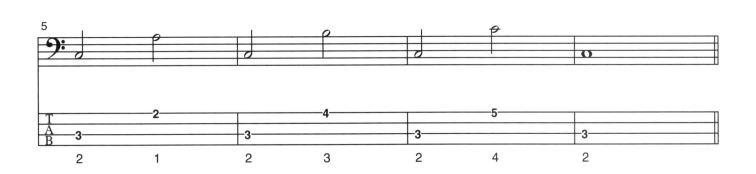

Chapter Six

Major Chords

When bass players play with other musicians they create bass lines from the *chords* the other musicians are playing. A chord is a group of three or more notes played together. To be able to create bass lines that work with the chords and are interesting and fun to play, you must learn about the different types of chords, starting with *triads*. A triad is a three-note chord.

The first type of triad we will learn about is the *major triad*. A major triad consists of the root (the note on which the triad is built, the tonic of a major scale), the 3rd and the 5th of the major scale.

The C Major Triad Related to the C Major Scale

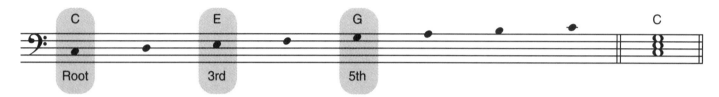

The chord symbol above the staff (see page 51) indicates which chord is being played. When a pianist or guitarist sees the chord symbol "C," they play the notes in the C Major chord (C–E–G). A major chord symbol is simply the letter name of the chord.

Major Triad Fingerings

The most basic way to build a bass line is to play an *arpeggio* of the chord. In an arpeggio, the notes of a chord are played one at a time. Here are three different ways to play the major triad on your bass. Fingerings 1 and 2 can be played on any two strings of your bass. Fingering 3 can be played starting on either the 3rd or 4th strings.

All three fingerings are moveable and can start on any note.

Fingering 1

Fingering 2

Fingering 3

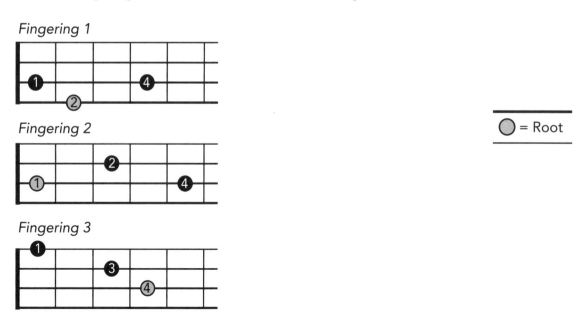

⬤ = Root

This bass line uses eighth notes and is created over a chord progression using major chords.

Note that all three fingerings are used to play the major chords in this tune.

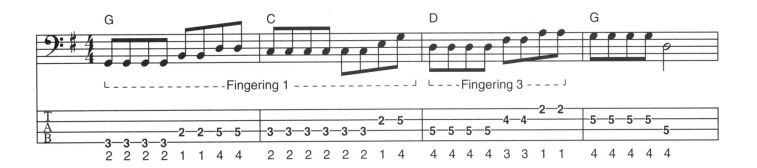

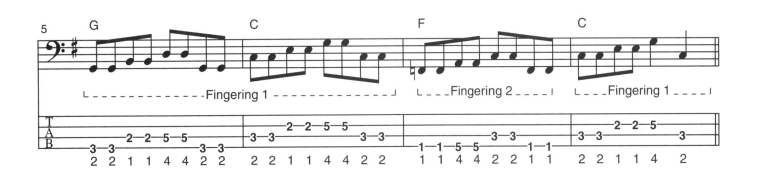

"Ever since I heard Stanley Clarke I have wanted to play the bass. It helps relieve the stress of the day and really helps me think more clearly as well as have fun."

Keith, 49
Company owner,
Aerospace part
manufacturer

Chapter Six

Minor Chords

A *minor triad* consists of the root, *minor 3rd* and a perfect 5th. Think of the minor 3rd as the lowered 3rd (♭3). So, if you take the 1, 3 and 5 of a major scale and lower the 3rd by a half step, you have a minor triad (1–♭3–5).

The C Minor Triad Related to the C Major Scale

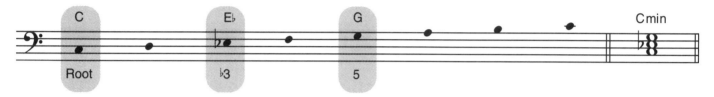

Minor Triad Fingerings

Here are three different ways to play the minor triad on your bass. Fingerings 1 and 2 can be played on any two strings of your bass. Fingering 3 can be played starting on the 3rd or 4th strings.

All three fingerings are moveable and can start on any note.

Fingering 1

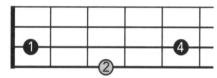

Fingering 2

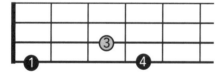

Fingering 3

Here is a common chord progression that uses both major and minor chords. The bass line uses chord tones of each chord.

Notice the different fingerings used to play the major and minor chords. The three fingerings for both the major and minor triad are used in this tune. Fingering 3 for each triad is referred to as an "extended fingering" and for this reason is not as practical or commonly used as the first two. Whenever possible, use Fingering 1 or 2 until you have more experience in playing the bass.

Major and Minor Chord Tune

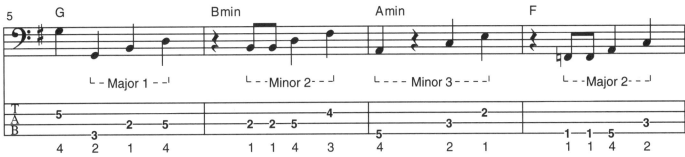

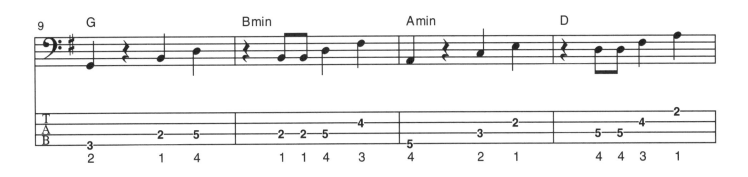

Chapter Six

Augmented and Diminished Chords

Augmented and *diminished* triads are not used with the frequency that major and minor triads are used, especially when playing in the styles of blues, rock, funk, reggae and other popular styles of music. It is, however, important to be aware of these chord types as you will most likely come across them at some point in your musical endeavors.

The diminished triad can be constructed by taking the 1, 3 and 5 of a major scale and lowering both the 3rd and the 5th a half step. The result is 1–♭3–♭5, or root, minor 3rd, diminished 5th.

The augmented triad can be constructed by taking the 1, 3 and 5 of a major scale and raising the 5th a half step. The result is 1–3–♯5, or root , major 3rd, augmented 5th.

The C Diminished Triad Related to the C Major Scale

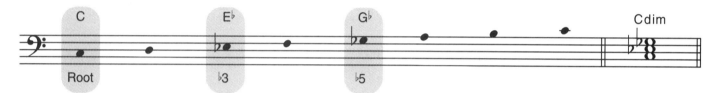

Diminished Triad Fingerings

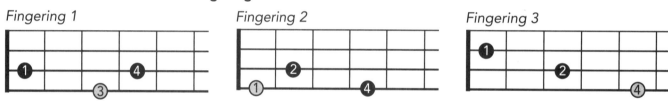

The C Augmented Triad Related to the C Major Scale

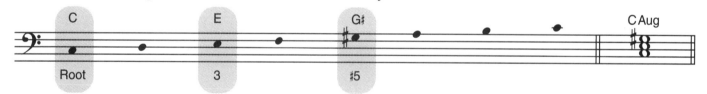

Augmented Triad Fingerings

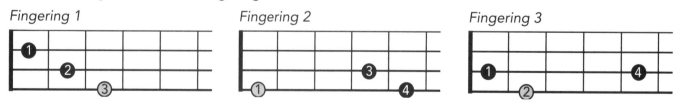

For a more in-depth understanding of major, minor, diminished and augmented triads, and how to create bass lines with them, check out *Beginning Electric Bass* (#19362) and *Musicianship for the Contemporary Bassist* (#21912).

Chords of the Major Scale

Many styles of music are at least partially characterized by certain chord progressions. These progressions are used in literally thousands of tunes. Understanding *diatonic harmony* will help you identify and become familiar with some of the most often-used chord progressions in blues, rock, funk and other popular styles of music. *Diatonic* means "belonging to the scale of the key;" *harmony* refers to chords. Diatonic harmony refers to chords built from a particular scale.

The Triads of the Major Scale

You have already learned the four types of triads. Now we will discuss the triads that are built on each degree of the major scale.

Each key has its own triads. Stacking diatonic 3rds (intervals of a 3rd using only notes from the scale) on each note of the scale creates these chords. Each triad is numbered according to the scale degree it is built upon. *Roman numerals* are used to indicate these degrees. For example, the triad built on the 5th degree of the scale is called the "five chord" and signified by the Roman numeral V.

Diatonic Triads in the Key of C Major

We create the diatonic triads by stacking two 3rds on each note of the scale. Some of the resulting triads are major, some are minor and one is diminished. Notice that uppercase Roman numerals are used for major chords and lowercase Roman numerals are used for minor chords.

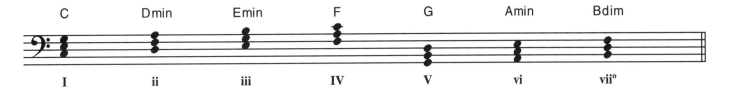

Note that:
I, IV and V are major
ii, iii and vi are minor
vii° is diminished

Roman Numerals:

I or i...............1	IV or iv..........4	VII or vii........7
II or ii............2	V or v.............5	
III or iii..........3	VI or vi..........6	

I–IV–V Chord Progression

A chord progression is the movement of one chord to another, or a series of chords. The I–IV–V chord progression is the most widely used chord progression in music and is the harmonic basis for many popular songs. Regardless of the style of music you want to play or what type of groove you prefer, becoming comfortable with the I–IV–V progression is essential. You will come across this progression at open mics, jam sessions, garage band rehearsals, world class blues shows and everywhere else on the face of the earth.

The I, IV and V chords are all major chords in any major key. For example, I, IV and V in the key of C Major are C (I), F (IV) and G (V).

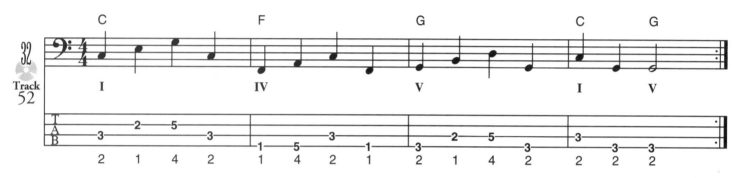

**Brian, 55
Supervisor,
Department of Labor**

"I wanted to play the bass the minute I saw The Kinks. I thought it was the coolest thing. I am always trying to get better as a bassist."

Beginning Bass for Adults

Here is a reggae bass line on a I–IV–V chord progression. Count carefully and pay attention to the rhythms.

This bass part is written with lots of open strings. After playing the tune through with open strings you can try to play the tune using closed notes wherever possible.

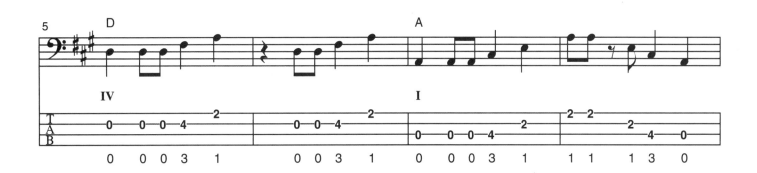

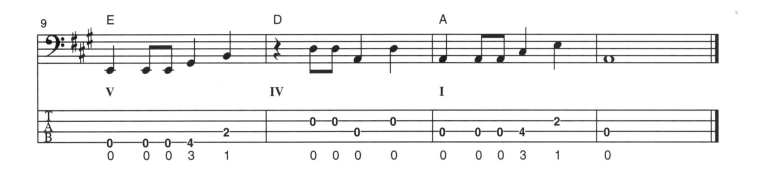

I–vi–IV–V Chord Progression

Like the I–IV–V chord progression, the I–vi–IV–V diatonic chord progression is used in literally thousands of tunes. Unlike the I–IV–V progression, this progression contains both major and minor chords. "Stand By Me" by Ben E. King and "Every Breath You Take" by The Police are good examples of songs written with the I–vi–IV–V chord progression.

This example shows arpeggios on the I–vi–IV–V chords in the key of C Major.

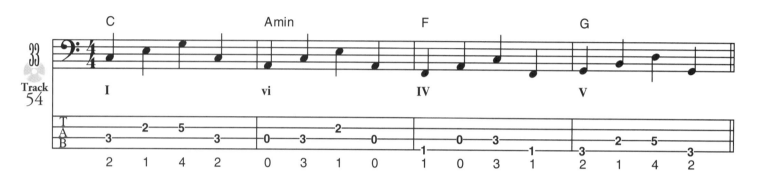

This example shows the I–vi–IV–V chords in the key of G Major.

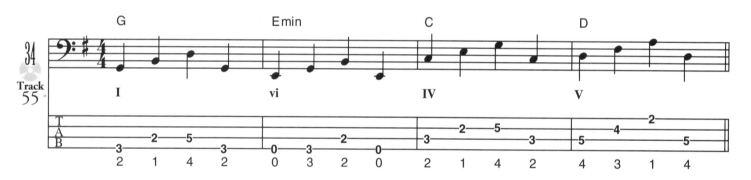

Beginning Bass for Adults

I–vi–IV–V
Bass Lines

This bass line is in the style of "Stand By Me," a well-known rhythm and blues tune. The line uses dotted quarter/eighth note rhythms and is created from the I–vi–IV–V chord progression.

Track 56

I–vi–IV–V in A

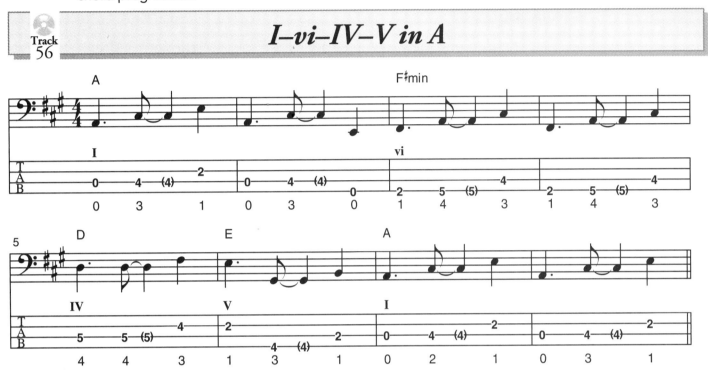

This bass line uses the same progression, but constant eighth notes completely change the groove.

Track 57

I–vi–IV–V Eighth-Note Boogie

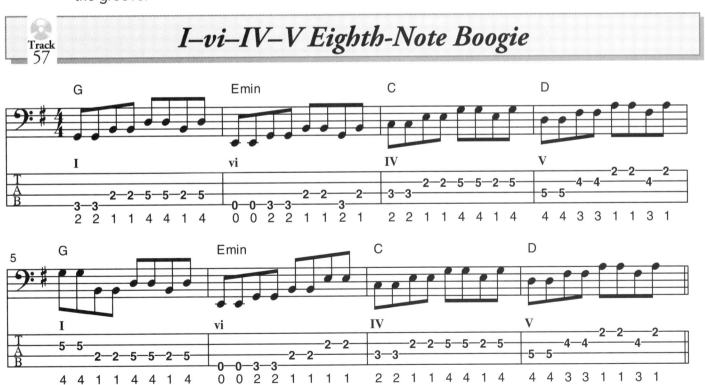

Chapter Seven

Introducing the Blues

The blues is one of the most popular and accessible styles of music. The most common blues form, the *12-bar blues*, is frequently used in other styles of music. From simple blues-rock tunes such as Chuck Berry's "Johnny B. Goode" to the more harmonically complex jazz-blues of Charlie Parker, the basic 12-bar blues form is the same. It is important for any bassist to become familiar with the blues—both its styles and its song form. The blues is the first thing that most musicians play when meeting for the first time at venues such as open mics and jam sessions. Learning blues bass lines will allow you to jam with many of your guitar and keyboard player friends.

Here is a 12-bar blues progression. In this progression the I chord is played for the first four bars.

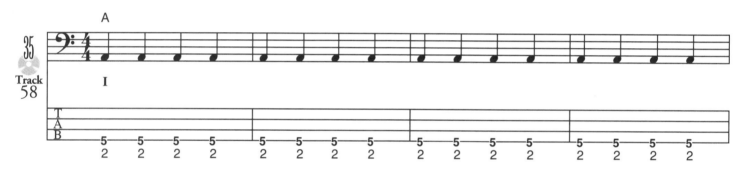

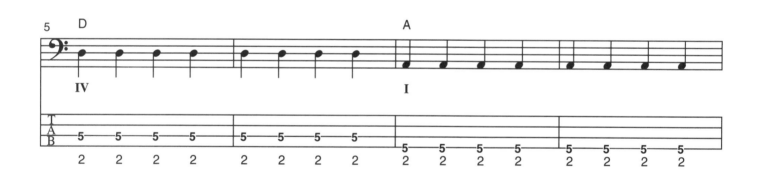

The Blues Quick Four

The 12-bar blues is a basic I–IV–V progression, but has variations. For example, although the I chord is often played for the first four bars, it is also common for the IV chord to be played in the second bar. Those familiar with the blues will often call this a *quick four*, or *quick change*.

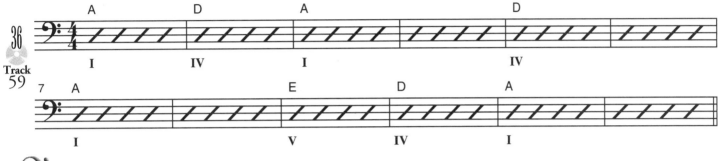

Blues Turnarounds

The last four bars of the blues is called the *turnaround*. It helps bring the progression back to the beginning when the form is repeating, usually by setting up the V chord in bar 12, which has a very strong pull back to I. Here are four turnarounds that are often played in the last four bars in a 12-bar blues. No. 4 is a jazz-oriented turnaround.

Chapter Seven

Major Pentatonic Scale

A *pentatonic scale* is a five-note scale. One of the most commonly used pentatonic scales used to create bass lines over major chords is the *major pentatonic* scale.

The major pentatonic scale uses 1, 2, 3, 5 and 6 of a major scale.

C Major Pentatonic Scale

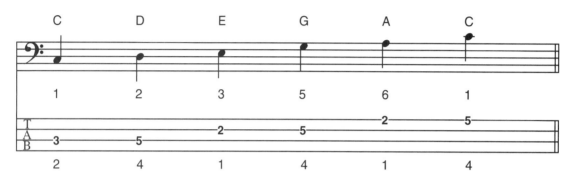

All of the fingerings below are moveable and can start on any note.

Fingering 1

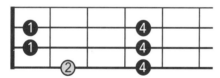

Fingering 2

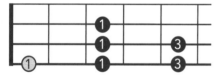

Fingering 3 (Two Octaves)

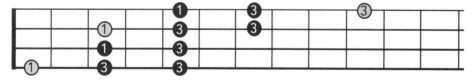

Rockabilly is a style of pop music marked by features of rock and country. The Stray Cats were one of the popular groups of this style.

This bass line uses quarter-note rhythms and notes from the major pentatonic scale for each chord. It can be heard on countless tunes. Practice slowly at first and when you have it, play along with the CD that is available with this book.

This bass line and those that follow are each created with a specific pattern of notes that can be transposed to any key. Repeated-pattern bass lines such as these are an important part of the blues style. When playing these pattern-based lines, the same fingering is often used to play the pattern over each chord in the form. This will be the case for most of the bass lines in this chapter.

Eight-note bass lines can be more rhythmically exciting than quarter note lines and help propel the music forward. It is a powerful musical feeling when the bass is locking in with a good drummer on eighth-note grooves with the volume up!

Here is the bass line with the same pitches you played in the last bass line, only with eighth-note rhythms. Be sure to count carefully and alternate the right-hand fingers.

Track
62

8th-Note Rockabilly

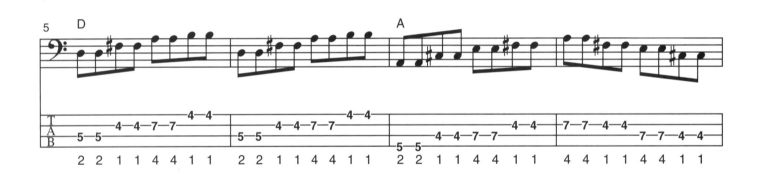

Dominant 7th Chords

Dominant 7th chords are commonly found in blues and funk music. If you want to be able to play great sounding bass lines that are fun to play in blues, funk and other styles, you should get to know your dominant 7th chords.

A dominant 7th chord is a four-note chord made with a major triad (refer to page 50) plus an additional 3rd above the 5th, which results in a *minor 7th* ($\flat$7) above the root. The scale degrees in a dominant 7th chord are R–3–5–$\flat$7.

The common chord symbols used for a C Dominant 7th are C7 and Cdom7. C7 is the more common of the two, and is the symbol we will use in this book.

The C Dominant 7th Chord Related to the C Major Scale

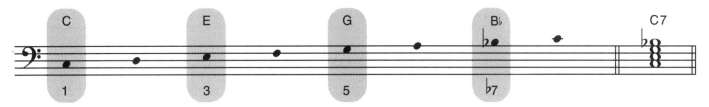

These fingerings are moveable and can start on any note.

Fingering 1

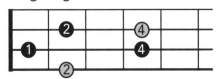

Fingering 2

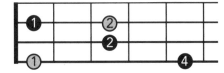

Fingering 3

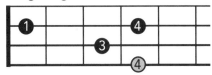

Notice that in this bass line, the same fingering pattern can be used for each chord.

This dominant 7th blues uses Fingerings 1 and 3 that you learned on page 65. Since Fingering 2 has a stretch, it is used less often.

Dominant 7th Rockabilly Groove

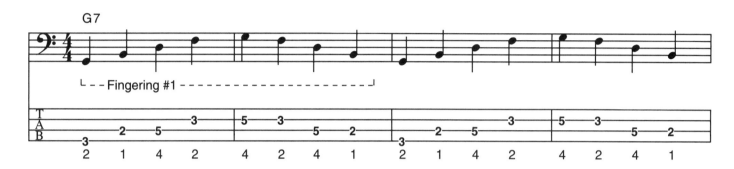

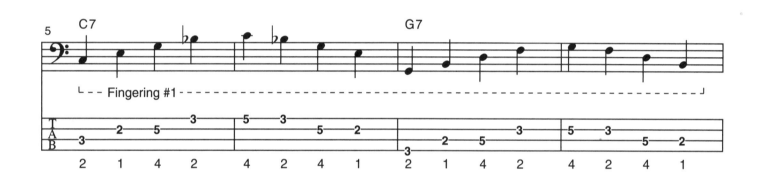

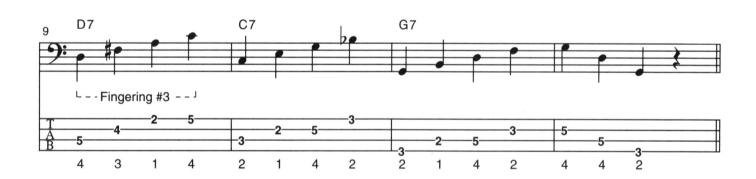

This bass line is similar to the one on page 66. Count carefully and alternate your right-hand fingers.

Swing Eighth Notes

Swing eighth notes, also known as *shuffle eighth notes*, are based on the eighth-note triplet (see page 47).

Here are four beats of eighth-note triplets.

Count: 1 & ah 2 & ah 3 & ah 4 & ah

Unlike a pair of straight eighths, the notes in a pair of swing eighths are not equal in duration. The first note is held longer than the second. They are similar in feel to an eighth-note triplet with the first two notes tied.

Here are the same eighth-note triplets with the first two notes of each triplet tied.

Count: 1 & ah 2 & ah 3 & ah 4 & ah

Swing eighths are written just like straight eighth notes. Over the next two pages, all of the bass lines are to be played with a swing eighth-note feel. You will find swing eighth indications (*Swing 8ths*) at the beginnings of the examples.

Here are four bars of swing eighth notes.

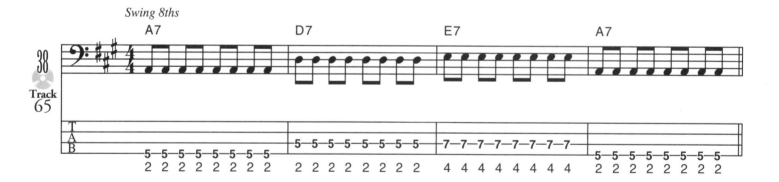

Swing Eighth-Note Blues Pattern

This bass line uses swing eighths and is played over 7th chords. Play the line slowly at first, then play along with the CD that is available with this book. This 12-bar blues uses the quick four and the turnaround ends with the V chord.

Track 66

Swingin' with 8ths

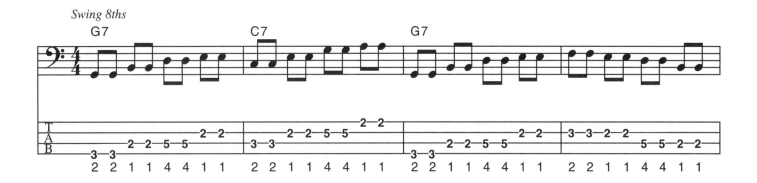

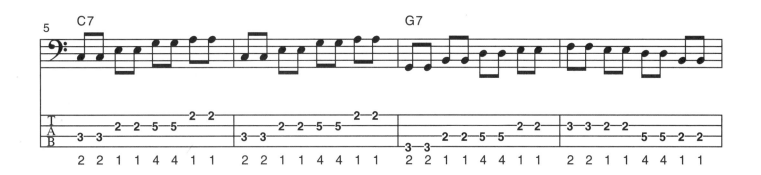

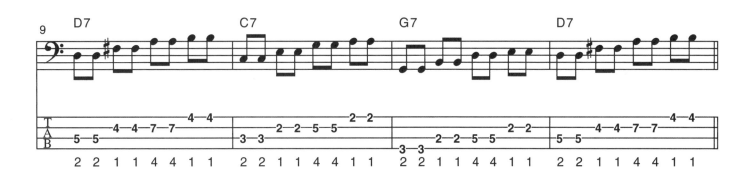

Blues-based tunes in blues and rock styles are often played in open-string keys such as E, A, D and G Major. In this chapter, you will find many of the bass lines written in these keys.

Chapter Seven

This blues bass line in the key of G Major uses a two-bar pattern over 7th chords in swing eighth notes. To accommodate the one-bar chords in the turnaround, the bass line uses the first bar of the two-bar pattern.

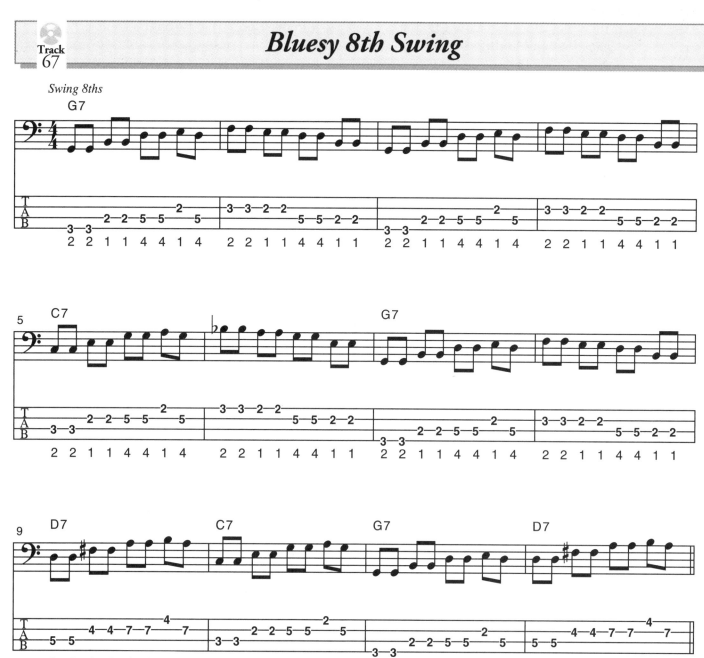

Bluesy 8th Swing

Track 67

Slow Blues

Many slow blues are written in $\frac{12}{8}$ time. In $\frac{12}{8}$ time, there are 12 eighth notes in a measure and, technically, the eighth note gets one beat. In reality, $\frac{12}{8}$ is felt as four beats with three eighth notes in each beat.

Slow blues tunes are often written in $\frac{4}{4}$ time with triplets.

Example

Here is how the above feel would be written in $\frac{12}{8}$ time.

The turnaround in a slow blues is often I–IV–I–V, as in the slow blues below. Notice that because the line is written in $\frac{12}{8}$, the dotted quarter note gets one beat (a dotted quarter equals three eighth notes).

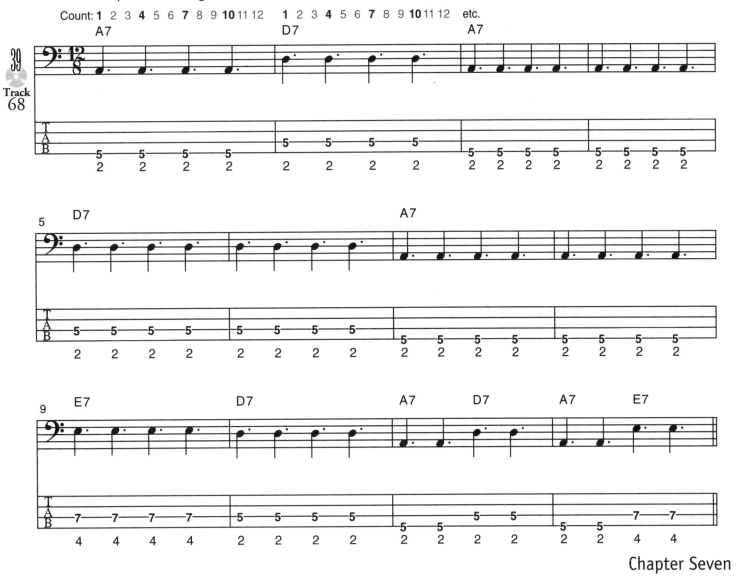

Chapter Seven

Have fun with this slow blues in the key of A. The quarter-eighth rhythm it uses sounds like swing 8ths would in $\frac{4}{4}$. Notice the I–IV–I–V turnaround is used. Count carefully.

Take It Slow

Count: **1** 2 3 **2** 2 3 **3** 2 3 **4** 2 3 etc.

16-Bar Blues

The *16-bar blues* is also a common song form. In a 16-bar blues, the I chord is used for the first eight bars. Listen to some Stevie Ray Vaughan recordings and you will be sure to find a few 16-bar blues tunes.

Track 70

16-Bar Blues in G

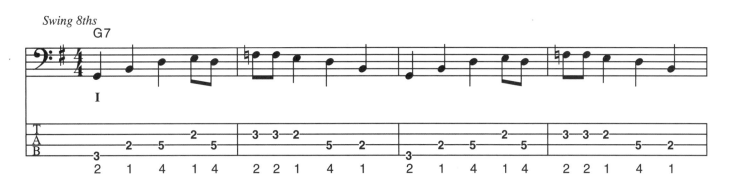

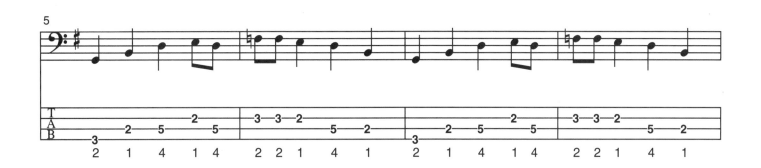

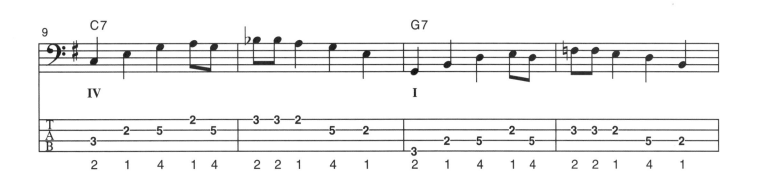

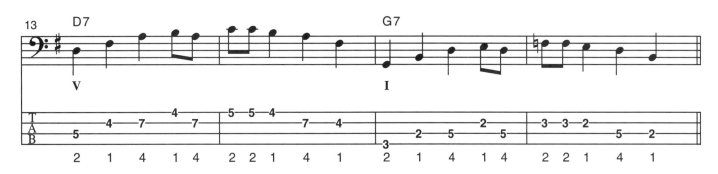

Chapter Seven

Blues Scale

The *blues scale* is used in many different styles of rock and is one of the primary ingredients in blues music. Musicians use the blues scale for melodies and solos.

The blues scale consists of scale tones 1, ♭3, 4, ♭5, 5 and ♭7.

C Blues Scale

Blues Scale Fingerings

All of these blues scale fingerings are moveable.

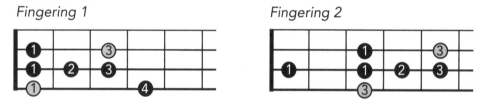

Fingering 1   *Fingering 2*

Fingering 3 (Two Octaves)

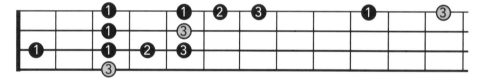

Bass players use the blues scale for bass lines on riff-oriented blues tunes.

C Blues Scale Riff

In this riff, the F♯ note in bars 1 and 3 are written as G♭ in measures 2 and 4. The F♯ and G♭ notes are located on the same fret on the bass. This is due to the direction of the line: sharps are usually used when ascending; flats are usually used when descending.

Beginning Bass for Adults

This bass line was created with the blues scale. Play it slowly at first and then gradually increase the tempo. Once you are comfortable with the line, have a friend play the chords with you or play along with the CD that is available with this book.

This bass line is constructed with a two-bar pattern. This means that the bass riff is two bars long and the same two-bar riff is used over each chord. The first bar of the pattern is used over one-bar chords.

If you want a more in-depth study of blues bass lines, check out the *Beginning Blues Bass* (#22561). This book gives you the tools to create blues bass lines and has a library of blues bass lines every bassist should have under their fingers.

Chapter Eight

Minor 7th Chord

A *minor 7th chord* is a minor triad plus a minor 3rd above the 5th (minor 7th or ♭7 above the root). The resulting scale degrees are 1–♭3–5–♭7. The chord symbols commonly used for C Minor 7 chords are Cmin7, Cmi7, Cm7 and C-7. Cmin7 and Cmin7 are the most commonly used symbols. In this book, we will use Cmin7.

The C Minor 7th Chord Related to the C Major Scale

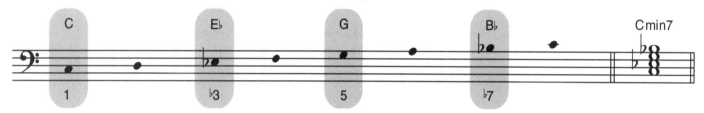

These fingerings are moveable and can start on any note.

Fingering 1

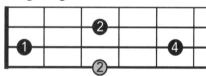

Fingering 2

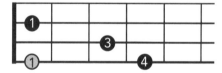

Fingering 3

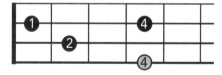

Here is a bass line in a reggae style using minor 7th chords. Have a guitar player friend play the chords as you play the bass line.

In this tune, only Fingering 2 of the three minor 7 chord fingerings is utilized, but all three fingerings will become useful as you become more experienced.

Reggae in A Minor

Track 73

The Dorian Mode

The *Dorian mode* is often used in blues, funk and jazz music. It is often used to create bass lines and melodies over minor triads and minor 7th chords. If you play a major scale starting and ending on the second degree, you get the Dorian mode. For example, if you play a C Major scale starting on the second degree, D, you get the D Dorian mode.

The scale degrees of the Dorian mode, compared to a major scale starting on the same note, are 1–2–♭3–4–5–6–♭7–8(1). In other words, if you lower the 3rd and 7th degrees of a major scale, you get the Dorian mode. Here is the C Dorian mode.

C Dorian Mode

Dorian Mode Fingerings

Here are two fingerings that can be used to play the Dorian mode.

Fingering 1

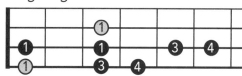

Fingering 2

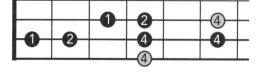

The Dorian mode is a mode of the major scale. To learn more about the major scale modes and how they are used to create bass lines, check out *Intermediate Electric Bass* (#19359) and *Musicianship for the Contemporary Bassist* (#21912).

Beginning Bass for Adults

This bass line is built on minor 7th chords and is created from the Dorian mode built on the root of each chord (G Dorian over Gmin7, C Dorian over Cmin7, etc.). Be sure to keep a steady count.

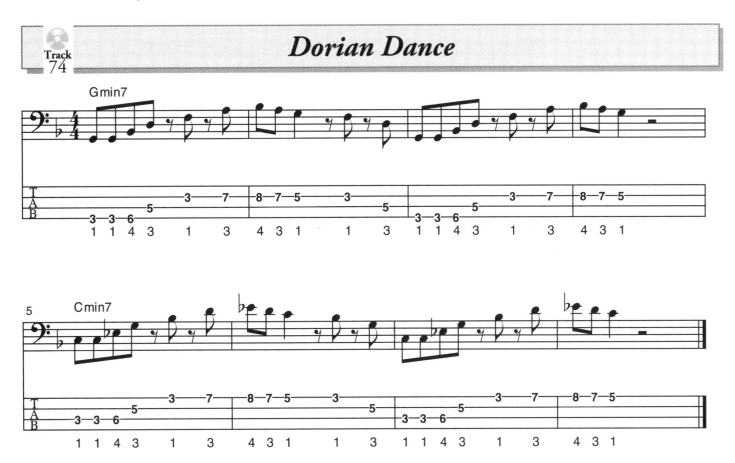

Notice that, since the A Dorian mode can be found by playing the G Major scale starting on the second note, A, the key signature for A Dorian is the same as the key signature for G Major: one sharp (F♯).

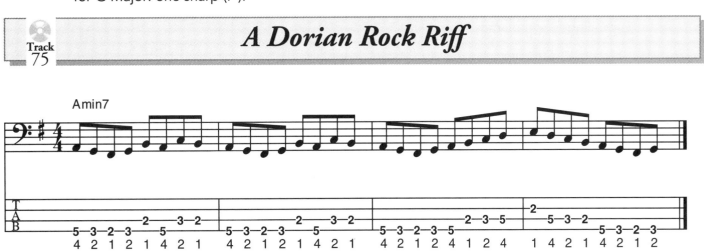

The Mixolydian Mode

The *Mixolydian mode*, like the Dorian mode, is a mode of the major scale. The Mixolydian mode can be created by playing a major scale starting on the 5th degree. For example, if you play a C Major scale starting and ending on its 5th degree (G), you have played the G Mixolydian mode.

The Mixolydian mode can also be thought of as a major scale with a $\flat 7$, hence the scale formula, 1–2–3–4–5–6–$\flat 7$–8(1).

C Mixolydian Mode

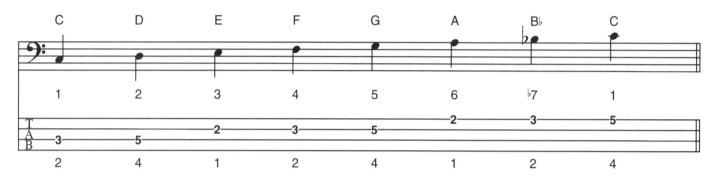

The Mixolydian mode is a useful scale for creating bass lines over dominant 7th chords. If you study the bass lines from Chapter Seven (page 60, the blues chapter), you'll find that most of the bass lines were created from the Mixolydian mode.

These fingerings are moveable.

Fingering 1

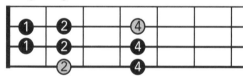

Fingering 2

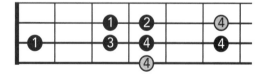

Mixolydian Riffs

These bass riffs are created from the Mixolydian mode and are played over dominant 7th chords.

Below is a bass line that you have probably heard played on many tunes. It is a boogie bass line based on the Mixolydian mode but also includes the minor 3rd interval. Listen to the bluesy effect of the dissonance (clashing sound) caused by playing a minor 3rd against a dominant 7th chord, which has a major 3rd (for example, the B♭ in bar 1 against a G7 chord).

Play this slowly at first, then play along with the CD that is available with this book if you have it.

There are different fingerings you can use to play this bass line. Try using the 4th finger and then try it with the 3rd, as shown below. In this fingering, note the diagonal line when using the 3rd finger to play two consecutive notes. This line indicates a slide; slide your 3rd finger along the string from one note to the next, making a gliding sound.

$\underset{\diagup}{\underline{SL}}$ = Slide

Track 78 — *Blues with Mixo*

Chapter Nine
funk

The feeling you get when you lock into a funk groove with a good drummer is one of the most rewarding aspects of being a bass player. Funk usually is played with only a few chords and sometimes even over just one chord. In this chapter we will touch on a couple of the many different techniques bassists can use when playing funk music.

Syncopation

Syncopation is the shifting of the accent to the weak part of the beat. For example, when we count eighth notes (1–&, 2–&, 3–&, 4–&), the numbered part of each beat, the onbeat, is the strong part of the beat. The "&" of each beat, the offbeat, is the weaker part of the beat. Emphasizing the onbeats results in syncopation. In an eighth-note funk bass line, inserting eighth rests on the onbeats makes it funky.

Here is an example of syncopation in an eighth-note funk line (with the syncopated notes circled).

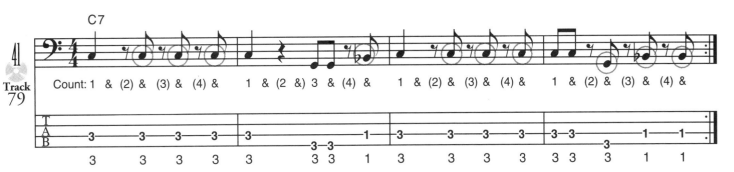

♩ = Syncopated note

Here's another syncopated eighth note line. Be sure to count carefully.

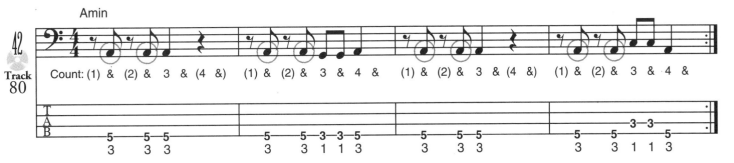

Often, a funk tune is based on one dominant 7th chord. You may hear someone call out "funk in E" at a jam session. Your bass line could be something like this.

Track 81

Funk in E

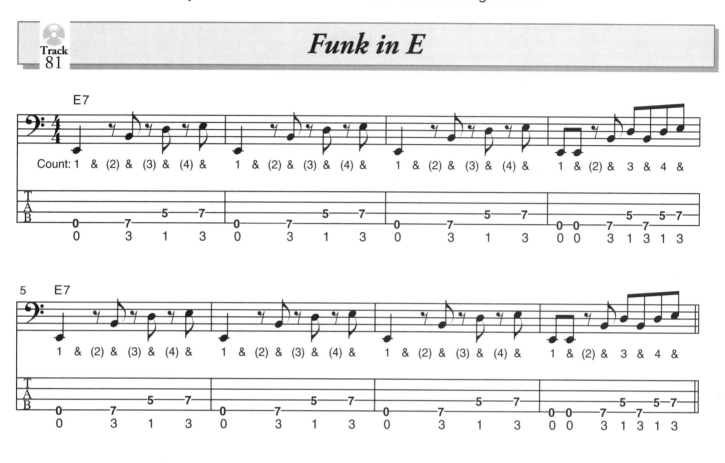

Here is a syncopated eighth-note bass groove over just two chords. Be aware that the fingering used for this bass line requires that you shift your hand.

Track 82

Funk for Two

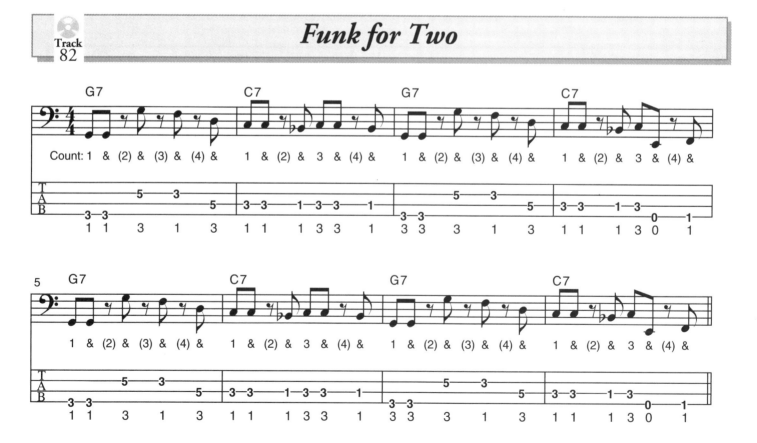

Beginning Bass for Adults

Sixteenth Note Rest

The *sixteenth rest* signifies silence for one quarter of a beat.

Here is a sixteenth rest.

Funk Groove with Sixteenth Note Rests

In a sixteenth-note funk bass line, the sixteenth rests commonly occur on the first and third subdivisions of the beat. In other words, when counting "1–e–&–ah, 2–e–&–ah," etc., the sixteenth rests would likely fall on numbers and "&."

This bass line has sixteenth notes and rests. Play the line slowly at first and be sure to count carefully. Also, remember to alternate the fingers of the right hand.

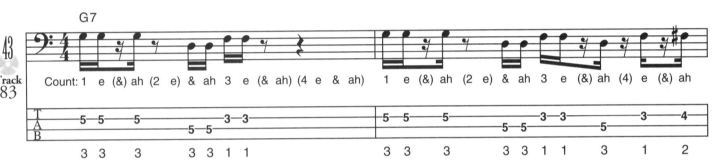

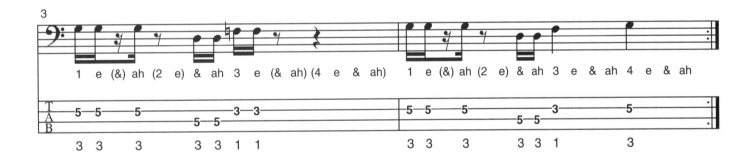

Muted Notes

The *muted* or *dead note* (×) is an integral part of funk bass playing. To produce a muted note, rest the fingers of the left hand on the strings (don't press them down to the fretboard) to prevent them from vibrating while plucking a string with the right hand. This will result in a percussive, almost unpitched sound. If you use just one finger to mute the string, there is a chance you may produce a tone. To be safe, use two or more fingers.

We call this style of funk, plucking the strings with the fingers of the right hand and using muted notes, *pizzicato funk*.

Muted Quarter Notes

Here are quarter note A notes played with the open 3rd string and then muted. The muted note is signified with the symbol.

Muted Eighth Notes

This example has eighth notes on the open 3rd string. Then, the notes on the offbeats are muted.

Muted Sixteenth Notes

In the second measure of this example, the last two sixteenths in each beat are muted.

Playing muted notes can be tricky. Play slowly at first to get the desired effect.

Play these bass lines slowly at first and make sure you get the effect of the muted notes. After you become comfortable with these bass lines, have a friend play the chords along with you, or play along with the CD available with this book.

Muted Note Funk

Track 85

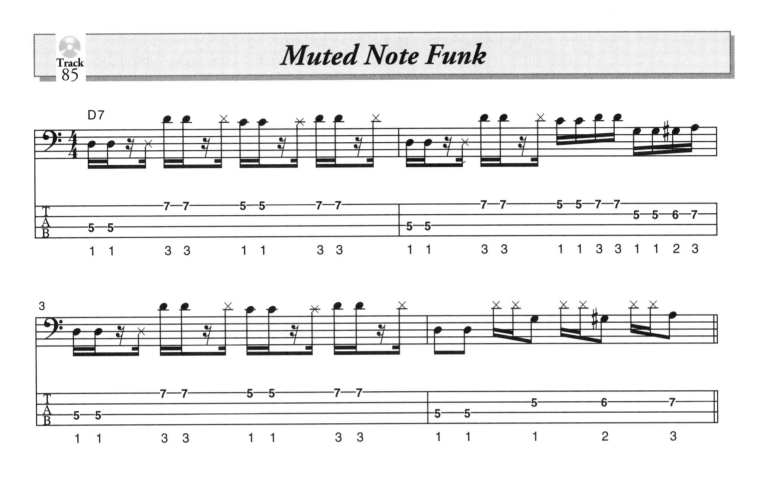

Muted but Heard

Track 86

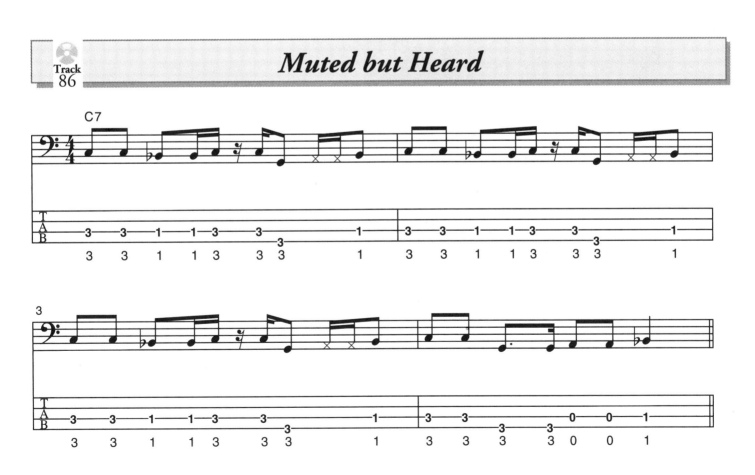

Chapter Nine

Introduction to Slap & Pop

The *slap & pop* style has evolved into one of the most exciting styles of electric bass playing. This chapter is designed to give you an introduction to the style. Although there are several techniques involved in the slap & pop style, we will focus on the two essential techniques: the *slap* and the *pop*.

The Slap

The slap is executed by using the lower side (heel) of the thumb to strike the string. After striking the string, allow the thumb to bounce off to prevent stopping the string from ringing. The trademark sound of the slap is a strong, percussive sound. It is also important to stop the string from ringing when you are done with the note to prevent any unwanted noise.

There are two common slapping positions used. Try both and use the one that is most comfortable for you.

Slap Position No. 1

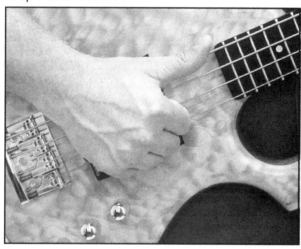

Slap Position No. 2

Play these examples slowly at first. Watch for the muted notes.

The symbol used to indicate the slap technique is "S." In the following examples all notes are to be played with the slap technique. Notice there are some muted notes.

Open-String Exercise on the 4th String

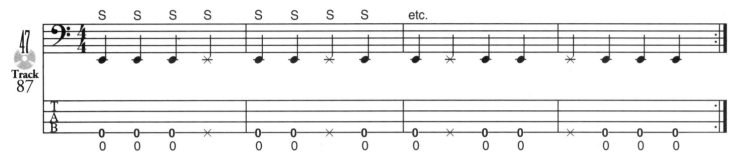

Open-String Exercise on the 3rd String

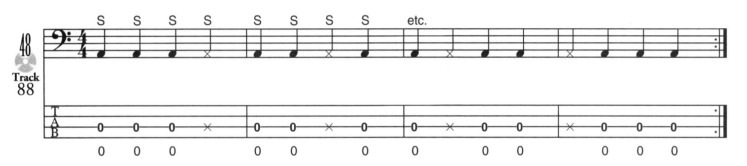

Open-String Exercise on the 3rd and 4th Strings

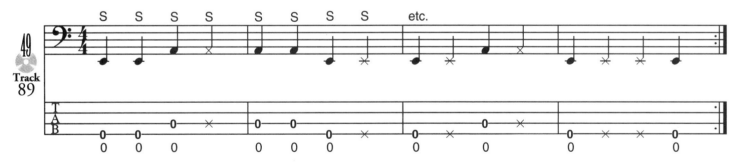

Slap Bass Lines

Here is a bass line that uses the slap technique. Pay close attention to the muted notes.

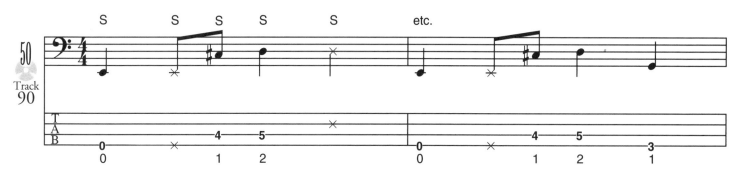

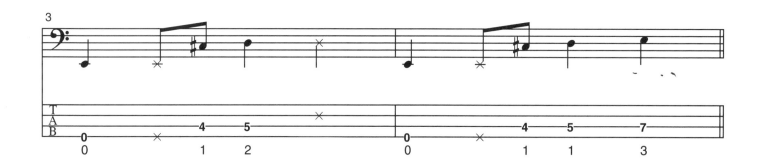

Here is another slap bass line. This one has consistent eighth notes. Play it slowly at first and gradually increase the tempo.

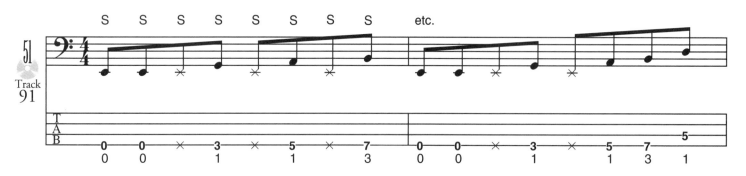

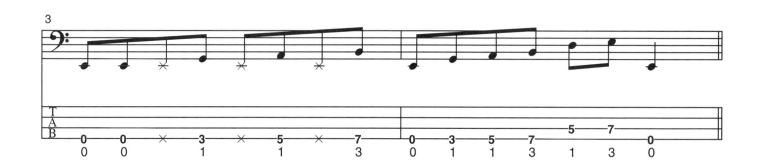

The Pop

The pop is a very distinct sound in the slap & pop style. A pop is executed by placing the index finger of the right hand underneath the string (usually the 1st or 2nd string) and pulling it away from the fretboard, allowing it to snap back against the frets. The pop produces a very percussive sound.

Below are pictures showing the two hand positions that can be used when popping strings.

Pop Position No. 1

Pop Position No. 2

The pop has an even more distinctive sound than the slap. The sound is usually more percussive than that of the slap. Experiment with both hand positions shown on page 91.

It is very common to pop a note an octave above a slapped note. You can use either the left-hand 3rd or 4th finger to fret the octave. For example, when you play an A note on the 5th fret of the 4th string, and pop the A an octave higher on the 7th fret of the 2nd string, you can use the 3rd finger, but many bassists prefer to use the 4th. Do whatever feels comfortable for you. Using the 4th finger will free your other fingers for muting and other techniques. The 4th finger is indicated for popped notes in the examples that follow, but you can substitute the 3rd if that is more comfortable for you.

Slap & Pop Exercise No. 1

Track 92

```
S   P   S   P   S   P   S   P   S   P   S   P   S   P   S   P
T-------7-------4-------|-------5-------6-------|-------7-------4-------|-------5-------6-------|
A-------|-------|-------|-------|-------|-------|-------|-------|-------|
B--5-------2-------|----3-------4-------|----5-------2-------|----3-------4-------|
  1   4   1   4   1   4   1   4   1   4   1   4   1   4   1   4
```

Slap & Pop Exercise No. 2

```
S   P   S   P   S   P   S   P   S   P   S   P   S   P   S   P
T-------7-------4-------|-------5-------6-------|-------7-------4-------|-------5-------6-------|
A-------|-------|-------|-------|-------|-------|-------|-------|-------|
B--5-------2-------|----3-------4-------|----5-------2-------|----3-------4-------|
  1   4   1   4   1   4   1   4   1   4   1   4   1   4   1   4
```

Slap & Pop Exercise No. 3

```
S   P   S   P   S   P   S   P   S   P   S   P   S   P   S   P
T-----------4-------|-------5-------6-------|-------7-----------|-----------|
A-------7-------|-------|-------|-------|-------|-------4-------|----5-------6-------|
B--5-------2-------|----3-------4-------|----5-------2-------|----3-------4-------|
  1   4   1   4   1   4   1   4   1   4   1   4   1   4   1   4
```

Beginning Bass for Adults

Slap & Pop Bass Lines

These bass lines use both the slap and the pop techniques. The notes that should be slapped are indicated with an (S) and the notes that should be popped are indicated with a (P).

Play these bass lines extremely slow at first, then when you are ready, play along with the CD that is available with this book.

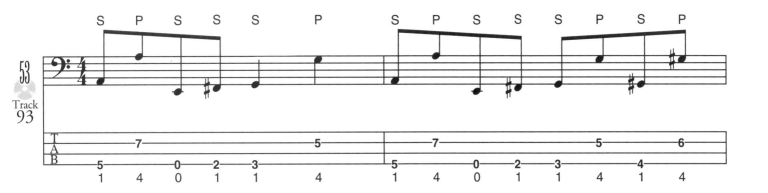

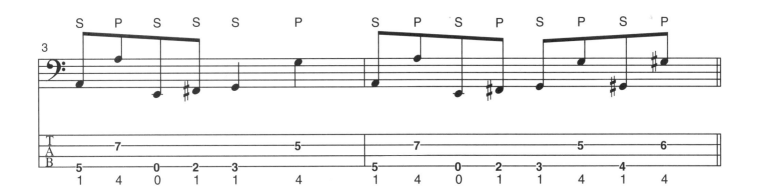

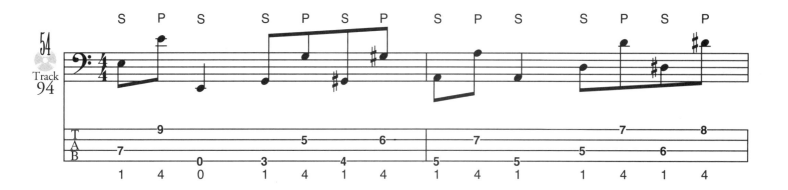

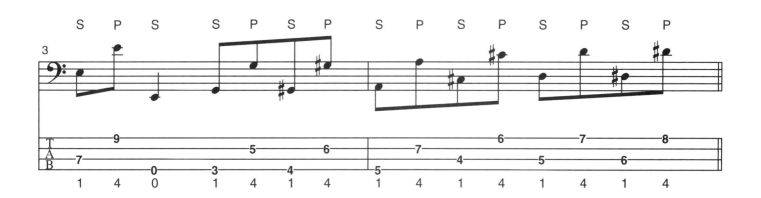

Beginning Bass for Adults

Slap & Pop
with 10ths

A 10th is the interval of a 3rd plus an octave.

Slap & Pop with 10ths

Here is a slap bass line with intervals of a 10th. Play the line slowly at first, then gradually increase the tempo. When you are comfortable with the line, play along with the CD that is available with this book.

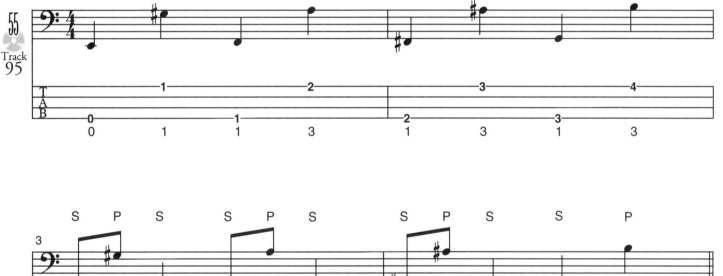

The bass lines in this chapter have been an introduction to the style of slap & pop bass playing. If you enjoy playing this style, you can get a much more in-depth look at the techniques involved in *Slap & Pop Bass* (#21904).

Congratulations! You have completed *Beginning Bass for Adults*. Don't stop learning now. The books listed on page 4 will help you on your way. Play with other people as often as you can, and listen to the many great bass players in all styles on recordings. We'll see you on the bandstand!

Chapter Nine

bass fingerboard chart

The Bass Notes in the First Octave

The following chart shows the positionof every bass note in the first octave (the first 12 frets).